Teaching with Vision

Teaching with Vision

Culturally Responsive Teaching in Standards-Based Classrooms

Edited by

Christine E. Sleeter
Catherine Cornbleth

Foreword by
Bill Bigelow
Linda Christensen

Teachers College
Columbia University
New York and London

Published by Teachers College Press, 1234 Amsterdam Avenue, New York, NY
10027

Library of Congress Cataloging-in-Publication Data

Teaching with vision : culturally responsive teaching in standards-based classrooms /
edited by Christine E. Sleeter, Catherine Cornbleth.
        p. cm.
    Includes bibliographical references and index.
    ISBN 978-0-8077-5172-5 (pbk. : alk. paper) — ISBN 978-0-8077-5173-2 (hard-
cover : alk. paper) 1. Effective teaching—United States. 2. Education—Standard—
United States. 3. Minorities—Education—United States. I. Sleeter, Christine E.,
1948–   II. Cornbleth, Catherine.
    LB1025.3.T4393 2011
    371.102—dc22

                                                                        2010046379

ISBN 978-0-8077-5172-5 (paperback)
ISBN 978-0-8077-5173-2 (hardcover)

Printed on acid-free paper

Manufactured in the United States of America

18 17 16 15 14 13 12   8 7 6 5 4 3 2

Contents

Foreword

A few years ago a new superintendent came to town in Portland, Oregon, where we each taught in public high schools for about 30 years. She was dubbed a "reformer," in today's upside-down world where words so often have come to mean their opposite. The superintendent complained in various forums that when it came to curriculum and professional development, "nothing had been done." That seemed curious to us because for years Portland teachers had collaborated to produce imaginative, lively, critical, and academically rigorous curriculum.

We came to realize through her tenure that what the superintendent meant by "nothing had been done" is that we had no uniform, standardized curriculum that had been imposed on teachers here. In Portland schools, there was no "one best system" mandated from the top. No doubt, like any large school district in a city of high unemployment and inequality, Portland had its share of problems. But the superintendent's solution to address these problems was not to reinvigorate and systematize teacher curricular creativity but to look to distant corporations for programs, scripts, and texts that could "fix" us.

Today, this struggle between grassroots, collaborative, culturally responsive teaching and a top-down, teach-by-the-numbers, do-it-or-else approach continues. And that's one reason why *Teaching with Vision* is such a welcome contribution. In this collection, Christine Sleeter and Catherine Cornbleth demonstrate that extraordinary things can happen when teachers recognize that teaching is not just a matter of following directions, but is an art that requires us to pay attention to our students' lives and to the world beyond. These stories offer inspiration and courage to teachers to resist the pressure to simply implement a cookie-cutter curriculum. Implicitly, they argue that teaching is an ethical act that requires us to "listen" to our students' lives—and to care about the social forces that influence our students' choices and challenges. These essays chronicle the work of teachers who are concerned not only about fidelity to state standards, but who also care about social justice.

Sleeter and Cornbleth selected teachers across grade and content areas, who, with elegance and honesty, "story" their classroom practice. Yes, they offer "hey, I could do that too" examples of imaginative teaching. But this collection of essays is more than a how-to manual of fine instruction; these voices from the classroom provide a curricular conscience. They demonstrate how we as teachers can "talk back" to the reform agenda currently in vogue among elected officials, big name foundations, corporate executives, and some educators. This agenda celebrates mandated curriculum that eras-es the race, class, gender, and place differences that make one-size-fits-all teaching so profoundly inappropriate. Sleeter and Cornbleth's collection of teacher vignettes pulls out chairs around a public school table for educa-tors to discuss classroom practice that is grounded in students' lives and is responsive to their academic needs. Through these teaching stories, they demonstrate the kind of rich intellectual life and curiosity that we need to create the schools our children deserve.

In *Teaching with Vision*, teachers from both sides of the country describe rich examples of classroom practice without resorting to the kind of needlessly obtuse jargon so regrettably common in educational writing. This work—from developing curriculum that honors the history of indig-enous groups to developing interdisciplinary units about agriculture in a farming community—is culturally sensitive, critically astute, and absolutely essential for teachers and teacher educators today.

This work defies the paced, scripted, cubicle-hatched curriculum that deskills teachers. These chapters show teachers who think, teachers who write, teachers who understand not only *what* they are teaching but who can articu-late *why*. As Sleeter and Cornbleth note, "Their stories rebuke the notion that there is one set of 'best practices' for everyone, everywhere." And it's that kind of reflection that moves us to change our strategies, our content—even our underlying premises—as the teachers in this volume do.

Books about "culturally relevant" teaching crowd our bookshelves, boast-ing more than they provide. *Teaching with Vision* doesn't boast, it doesn't strut; it delivers both theory and practice on how to construct lessons that take into account students' lives and curricular needs. This book dares to ask educators to be curricular artists, architects, and craftspeople. Teachers here construct math curriculum, history units, and writing topics instead of obedi-ently teaching the paralyzed lessons produced by people far removed from the rural areas or cities where they work and their students live.

What we need in these tough times are stories of teachers who put their students first, who seek ways to teach about what matters, and who don't simply look for quick fixes to boost test scores. *Teaching with Vision* sug-gests that we need to put classrooms and teacher creativity at the center of any discussion of school reform.

Bill Bigelow
Linda Christensen

Introduction

We created this book primarily for new teachers (including prospective or preservice teachers)—especially those who may be working in less than ideal or supportive circumstances. New teachers today, such as yourself, face a set of challenges that can make learning to teach well particularly difficult. On the one hand, as you are probably well aware, classrooms are increasingly diverse ethnically, racially, linguistically, socioeconomically, and in other ways. You *can* learn to teach diverse groups of students well, but doing so does not come naturally. On the other hand, too many professional development efforts, and maybe even your own preservice teacher education program, emphasize learning to use curriculum packages or scripted programs, following curriculum standards and pacing guides, and administering tests. In such procedurally or management-oriented professional development, attention to students is diminished or lost altogether. As a new teacher, you may find yourself struggling to make your teaching inspiring, creative, and culturally responsive, as well as successful in terms of promoting students' achievement as measured by their test scores.

Add to this the need for a knowledgeable, ethical, and creative citizenry who can address a broader set of social concerns, such as the growing gap between rich and poor, shrinking global resources among burgeoning populations, and global climate change, and teachers can feel overwhelmed. We are particularly concerned that standards—or assessment-based and standardized approaches to teaching and professional development—leave new teachers with few models of culturally responsive, intellectually engaging, socially aware teaching. Younger teachers today probably do not know first-hand what teaching, learning, and schooling were like before the deluge of standards and testing beginning in the mid-1980s. It is too easy to assume that the way things are, here and now, are the way they have to be, or the way they should be.

This book offers you the professional experience and wisdom of practicing teachers who have been navigating standards- and test-driven teaching environments without losing a vision of what teaching could and, we believe, should be. In this book, public school teachers who are diverse in backgrounds, schools and school levels, subject areas, and specialties talk with you about their practice. Rather than giving admonitions to "do it" or disembodied "how-to-do-its," these experienced teachers talk about actually "doing it," teacher to teacher. They write from the context in which they teach, explaining how they have dealt with challenges in those contexts.

1

They share with you some of their failures and struggles, showing how they learned from those struggles to enact the kind of teaching they believe in.

Their stories rebuke the notion that there is one set of "best practices" for everyone, everywhere. At the same time, they base their work on principles that outstanding teachers share:

- Demonstrating respect and caring for students and a sense of humor, along with commitment to meaningful teaching-learning
- Getting to know students and connecting academic learning with their experiences
- Reorganizing subject-matter content to make it more accessible and meaningful to students
- Being proactive and resourceful
- Being persistent and taking informed risks to benefit students
- Viewing problems or obstacles as challenges; being a trouble-shooter.

Teaching with Vision offers an antidote to standardization and invasive/ pervasive testing; in so doing, it offers grounds for hope.

In this introduction, we lay out some of the challenges and available evidence for making informed choices toward visionary teaching. We are encouraged by those teachers who work around, not just with and within, school, district, and state policy constraints. There simply is no "one best way" of teaching all things to all students in all times and places. While acknowledging cross-currents that prod teachers in different, sometimes contrary directions such as increasing diversity among students and curricular-instructional standardization (e.g., Cornbleth, 1995; Sleeter, 2005), we focus on extending culturally responsive, intellectually engaging, and socially aware teaching in the real world of schools that offer less than ideal or supportive settings for teaching and learning.

CULTURALLY RESPONSIVE TEACHING

Researchers and practitioners have long sought out "strong methods" of teaching that presumably would overcome differences among students, schools, and communities. Today, the search is for "best practices," a search that assumes that one size fits all. Recently, one of us was talking with some new teachers in an urban school. They expressed confidence in their preparation for teaching because they knew what the "best practices" were, and had studied the latest book describing them. But best practices for what? And for whom? As these new teachers considered such questions, it became apparent that their knowledge of their students' backgrounds was limited, as were their strategies for building instruction on what their students bring to the classroom. What they had learned about "best practices," although useful (such as designing instruction around inquiry), was limited.

The emergence of culturally responsive (or relevant) teaching theory, research, and practice over the past 30 years has challenged but not superseded presumably universal "best practices." Early work sought to improve the learning of indigenous students with culturally appropriate or congruent pedagogy that incorporated home "language interaction patterns" into classroom practice (see Ladson-Billings, 1995 for a historical overview). Later work moved beyond a language focus and success in school to consideration of students' cultural identity and critical thinking; in the United States, it also directed attention to additional groups of elementary school students, especially African American and Latino/a students, who might benefit from culturally responsive teaching (see, e.g., Gay, 2000; Villegas & Lucas, 2002). We should point out that the concept of culturally responsive teaching applies not just to students of color, but to everyone. The problem is that what is culturally responsive for White middle-class students passes as the norm, labeled simply as "good teaching" or "best practices." However, "best practices" and culturally responsive teaching are not necessarily mutually exclusive. One can adapt presumably best practices to specific groups of students. Alternatively, it could be argued that best practices are culturally responsive and, therefore, not universal but situation specific.

Ladson-Billings (1994, 1995) emphasizes that culturally responsive teaching is not simply intended to help marginalized students "fit in" to schools as they are and increase their test scores. Rather, its purposes and criteria are to provide opportunity and support for students to

- Learn meaningful academic knowledge, skills, and dispositions
- Affirm their cultural identity and heritage
- Become more critically aware and prepared to challenge inequities in and beyond school.

Gay's (2000) view of and guidelines for culturally responsive teaching emphasize

> using the cultural knowledge, prior experiences, frames of reference, and performance styles of ethnically diverse students to make learning encounters more relevant to and effective for them. It teaches *to and through* the strengths of these students. It is culturally *validating and affirming.* (p. 29, emphasis in original)

More specifically, culturally responsive teaching "acknowledges the legitimacy of the cultural heritages of different ethnic groups, both as legacies that affect students' dispositions, attitudes, and approaches to learning and as worthy content to be taught" (p. 29). It "builds bridges of meaningfulness between home and school experiences as well as between academic abstractions and lived sociocultural realities" (p. 29) and does so using varied resources and multiple perspectives in order to make meaningful academic learning and school success accessible to all students.

Culturally responsive teaching by definition is contextualized and tailor-made for particular students and student groups. Irvine (2003) describes culturally responsive teachers who

> understand and appreciate students' personal cultural knowledge and use their students' prior knowledge and culture in teaching by constructing and designing relevant cultural metaphors and images in an effort to bridge the gap between what the students know and appreciate and new knowledge or concepts to be mastered. (p. 68)

Culturally responsive teaching requires teachers who are working toward becoming skillful cultural mediators or brokers who can explain new concepts or challenge misconceptions with examples and illustrations from students' everyday lives.

The research on culturally responsive teaching with a focus on African American students has expanded (e.g., Lynn, 2006; Ware, 2006), and there is a growing literature about culturally responsive teaching with Mexican American and English language learners (ELLs) or bilingual students (e.g., Gutstein, Lipman, Hernandez, & de los Reyes, 1997; Sleeter, 2005). We have examples of culturally responsive teaching units (e.g., Irvine & Armento, 2001), guidance for learning about students' homes and communities (e.g., González, Moll, & Amanti, 2005; Villegas & Lucas, 2002), and subject-area-specific studies such as those in mathematics (e.g., Cahnmann & Remillard, 2002).

Earlier we mentioned that what commonly passes for good teaching grows from and responds to the culture of White middle-class mainstream students. What if educators extended the insights of culturally responsive teaching to the broader range of students in contemporary classrooms who differ from the mainstream White middle class, not only in terms of race or ethnicity, social class, and language but also religion, sexual orientation, cultural practices, physical or mental abilities, academic background, and motivation to do well in school? Santamaria (2009), for example, juxtaposes culturally responsive teaching and differentiated instruction, the latter often associated with inclusion classrooms, in an effort to identify complementary and hybrid teaching practices that attend to academic, cultural, linguistic, and socioeconomic diversity among students in two elementary schools.

The teachers whose voices we hear in the chapters that follow are culturally responsive in a myriad of ways—even though most do not use the language of culturally responsive teaching. As you will see, these teachers get to know their students as individuals and as group members, show respect for students and their cultures (thus affirming their identity and heritage), and connect meaningful academic teaching and learning with students' prior experiences. Some also encourage students (and their families) to become more critically aware and able to challenge inequity within and beyond school.

INTELLECTUALLY ENGAGING TEACHING

We use the terms *engaging* or *engagement* to refer to active student involvement that is "minds-on," not simply hands-on. Students are not merely listening or watching or completing a rote drill and practice worksheet. They are thinking about something intriguing or puzzling or otherwise challenging that they want to figure out. Why, for example, does a cup of water in liquid form take up more space when it freezes? What is lake-effect snow? Why does Chicago, Illinois, get little or no lake-effect snow while Buffalo, New York, gets a lot? Intellectual engagement also means that students are working with ideas in some way, alone or in combination with tangible objects. For example, what does fairness mean? When is it not fair to treat everyone the same?

You may be wondering—wasn't the purpose of the push for standards to raise the level of academic learning and thinking that happens in classrooms? If the new standards are supposed to be preparing everyone for the 21st century, shouldn't intellectual engagement be a given? This question is a good one, but the paradox is that, in many classrooms and schools—particularly those with low achievement test scores—students are slogged through memory work hour after hour, day after day. We have watched students become bored in such classrooms. When students are bored, not only do they not learn much, but they find other ways to entertain themselves, which their teachers experience as "discipline problems." As you will see in the teachers' stories, once students are actually intellectually engaged, the need for behavior management declines, and student achievement increases.

Clearly, culturally responsive teaching and intellectually engaging teaching can and should be mutually supporting, but one is not a guarantee of the other. Teaching with a focus on rote memorization of cultural information, such as memorizing a section of the Koran, Old Testament, or one of Shakespeare's plays, may be culturally responsive but is unlikely to be intellectually engaging. If, however, students were asked to analyze and interpret (or figure out the message of) song lyrics or poems from different traditions or parts of the world, cultural responsiveness serves intellectual engagement. For example, secondary students also could be asked to work in small groups to construct multiple interpretations of excerpts from the Koran, Old Testament, or Shakespeare.

Intellectually engaging teaching is for all students, meeting them wherever they are, and building on whatever they already know or understand. Just about all students can handle intellectual work if they understand the language, examples, and questions. As just one illustration, even second graders (and probably kindergarteners and first graders) understand perspective and multiple perspectives within their range of experience. Consider asking students to imagine a scenario in which two classmates are fighting at the back of the room. The teacher breaks up the fight and questions each student individually about what happened. Ask the class whether the two students are likely to offer the same story or version of events. Follow up by asking why or why not and what this might mean for other situations.

Researchers consistently find links between teacher expectations and student race and class background. Teachers commonly see students who are White and Asian as easier to challenge intellectually than those who are Black and Latino, and, similarly, students of middle- or upper-class backgrounds as easier to challenge intellectually than those from lower-class backgrounds. These reactions are based on teachers' beliefs about the extent to which parents value education (Hauser-Cram, Sirin, & Stipek, 2003; Pang & Sablan, 1998; Warren, 2002). But the truth is that students of color, English language learners, students who have learning disabilities, or students who come from lower-socioeconomic-status families do benefit from more, not less, intellectually engaging teaching. The work of Henry Levin and others on "accelerated" schools (e.g., Bloom, Ham, Melton, & O'Brien, 2001; Levin, 1988) well demonstrates that enrichment is not just for the supposedly gifted or already privileged. In fact, it may be more beneficial to those who often receive less. Another program of research that supports academically engaging teaching comes from a research group at the University of Wisconsin. Across grade and achievement levels, high school social studies students reported that challenging tasks involving higher-order thinking were more engaging compared to less challenging tasks (e.g., Newmann, 1990; Stevenson, 1990).

When we expect more of our students and act in ways that help them meet our expectations, they accomplish more (e.g., Comer, 1988; Diamond, Randolph, & Spillane, 2004; Ladson-Billings, 1994; Meier, 2002; Perry, Steele, & Hilliard, 2003; Reyes, Scribner, & Scribner, 1999). Intellectual challenge is not "borrring" or frustrating when students are guided and supported to tackle and meet the challenge. For example, one of our university students, a secondary social studies teacher, discovered that when he aimed to help students pass the state exam, fewer students passed than when he aimed to help students score at least 85% on the exam. Visionary teachers aim high.

SOCIALLY AWARE TEACHING

Socially aware teaching is based on the idea that education is a resource for the public good, particularly in a democratic society. This is not a new idea; John Dewey (1944) was one of its early advocates in the United States. Dewey wrote of the need to address the tension between the cultivation of shared common interests, and valuing the diverse experiences and perspectives of society's members:

> A society which makes provision for participation in its good of all its members on equal terms and which secures flexible readjustments of its institutions through interaction of the different forms of associated life is in so far democratic. Such a society must have a type of education which gives individuals a personal interest in social relationships and control, and the habits of mind which secure social changes without introducing disorder. (p. 99)

Educating young people for democratic participation in a diverse society entails fostering habits that enable them to hear and engage with diverse perspectives, including those that are routinely marginalized, and to practice working for justice.

Education these days is usually framed as preparation for work—or for doing well on tests. But the main premise underlying today's testing is that schools exist to prepare young people for the needs of the economy. What about the needs of a diverse and often highly fractured public? Where do students learn to engage across diverse points of view and experiences, if not in school? Where do they learn to think intelligently about public social problems like how might we work out better and more equitable ways of distributing social resources such as quality health care or education? Bigelow (2009) explains, "the entire effort to create fixed standards violates the very essence of multiculturalism," which can be thought of as "a 'conversation among different voices,' in the words of Henry Louis Gates, to discover perspectives that have been silenced" (p. 54), a point that echoes Ladson-Billings's discussion of culturally responsive pedagogy.

A socially aware education is grounded in a value for human rights. Carter and Osler (2000), for example, propose the UN Convention on the Rights of the Child as the basis for social education. They argue that when teachers explicitly work to build community in their classrooms, and engage children in the process of democratically working through classroom problems, children begin to develop respect for human rights. When teaching across differences is grounded in human rights, teaching and learning can be very powerful. For example, Fine, Weis, and Powell (1997) analyzed a world literature classroom in which students and adults learned to speak openly and honestly about difficult issues related to race, racism, and power.

The teachers worked hard to create safe spaces in which differences could be not only acknowledged, but openly interrogated. Although on some days classroom life was uninspiring, and on other days it was very difficult, "these classrooms, teachers, and students are mostly magic—the magic of imagining and creating a world that does not yet exist, a world in which difference is lifted and complicated" (p. 275).

Ultimately, socially aware teaching recognizes and grapples with the political ideology that is inherent in education, whether recognized or not. Framing education only in terms of the needs of the economy and curriculum as preparation for tests hides its political dimension. As Freire (1998) wrote, all education is political; there is no ideologically neutral education. "From the perspective of the dominant classes, there is no doubt of course that educational practice ought to cover up the truth and immobilize the classes" (p. 91). Socially aware teaching opens up political issues, allowing students to learn to examine issues for themselves. And it is possible to do so. For example, based on a study of three classroom teachers, Marri (2005) found permeability between disciplinary knowledge and critical multicultural education that would allow teachers to open up critical perspectives if they knew how to do so. The permeability can be found in teaching multiple perspectives and critical thinking, which are commonly valued in disciplinary curriculum. Although the teachers he studied taught critical thinking and multiple perspectives, they did not appear to have developed a vision that would enable them to teach "about and for a multicultural democracy" in as much depth as is possible.

Does socially aware teaching "work"? This is a difficult question to answer, because evaluating education based on how well it serves a diverse public, diverse communities, and the public interest cannot be directly measured. We can assess students' learning, but that is different from tracing what kinds of citizens they become. As Deborah Meier (2004) suggests, perhaps the impact of socially aware teaching is best judgedusing multiple indices of the well-being of a community and society, such as the thoughtfulness of its citizens. Ironically, however, and in the shorter term, when a socially aware teacher engages students academically, students do learn more. Both of us have observed a positive impact on their academic achievement.

ORGANIZATION OF THIS BOOK

The chapters that follow are organized into five parts, each of which interweaves the three themes we have discussed with the goal of supporting visionary teaching. Part I speaks to orienting oneself as a teacher to "real-world" schools. Eric Mohammed and Regina Forni each describe going into teaching with an idea of what it would be like, then experiencing the shock of discovering that students and schools were far from what they expected. After being knocked down by reality, they each went through a process in which they eventually learned to build visionary teaching for themselves.

Part II focuses on learning to learn from one's students, which is critical to visionary teaching. Secondary school teacher Frank DiLeo takes us into his ELL class, and shows how his teaching went from disastrously boring to exciting and inspired, as he learned to build on his students' lives. Elementary teacher Mike Roberts draws us into discussions about racism that his students initiated, showing us how he learned from his students to support such discussions.

In Part III, three teachers share how they learned to work creatively with curriculum and pedagogy within prescribed standards and procedures. First-grade teacher Kathy Richman shares a wonderful interdisciplinary unit about agriculture that she teaches almost every year, and discusses how she links it with the state standards, a link that was crucial to her being allowed to create curriculum rather than having to follow the adopted texts. Second-grade teacher Juanita Perea discusses the process she went through as she shifted away from following a fairly scripted reading/language arts package to develop several exciting projects with her Mexican immigrant students. High school math teacher Stephen Stiller shares a method he struggled to develop for hooking his students on math.

Part IV looks at connections between school and community. Joanne Rickard-Weinholtz explains the importance of ethnic identity from the point of view of members of the Tuscaroran nation, and tells us how she expanded her curriculum to base part of it in the local community. Gina DeShera shares what she has learned about the power of bringing the community and its issues into the classroom, as well as taking ourselves as teachers comfortably and authentically into the community where we teach.

Part V steps outside of the classroom to consider the kinds of support that enable visionary teachers to persist, especially in difficult circumstances. Janet Johns shares *Abriendo Caminos*, a professional development program she developed to support teachers' use of culturally relevant curriculum for ELLs in secondary schools. Finally, a group of teachers called Educators Advocating for Students tells their story of organizing as a teacher network to resist "one size fits all" teaching and support the kind of visionary teaching this book is about.

Christine E. Sleeter
Catherine Cornbleth

PART I

Orienting Yourself

Ideally, novice teachers would begin teaching in schools that are led by leaders who themselves have a rich vision of teaching and learning. However, if novice teachers are placed in high-poverty schools, the reality is that these schools are most likely to be under heavy pressure to raise test scores, and to require teachers to teach to standards and tests in order to do so. Principals may buffer that pressure, but they themselves are also under pressure.

Ideally, novice teachers would be mentored by excellent teachers through their first years of teaching, so they do not have to work through the nuts and bolts of visionary teaching by themselves. However, the reality is that they may not have a mentor at all, let alone an excellent one. Only half the states in the United States provide state-supported mentoring for new teachers, 40% of states have standards for selecting and preparing mentors, and only two states reduce new teachers' workload so they can participate in mentoring and induction activities (Akiba & LeTendre, 2009). With an absence of supporting conditions, learning from other teachers who have "been there" may be a new teacher's professional lifeline.

Excellent teachers who work in "real-world" schools located in high-poverty communities often describe going through a process of shock, then learning, as they encounter and work through what is often a gulf between how they had envisioned teaching and the realities they experience. For example, Brian Schultz (2008) describes his reaction to his first days teaching in the Cabrini Green ghetto of Chicago:

> Despite having dreams of making my classroom an experiential haven, when I actually entered the school on the first day, I realized teaching was much more difficult and complex than I had anticipated. After the first few days, I was not sure I would make it. More than once I contemplated quitting and never returning. The students knew how to push my buttons, and they tested me to see if I had what it took to endure. (p. 18)

The shock Schultz experienced had several dimensions. He is White and his students were African American; he had grown up in a professional-class community and his school was located in a very poor community; the school itself was very rundown, with terribly inadequate facilities and resources; and even though innovation and creativity were espoused values, teachers were mainly expected to raise students' test scores by delivering scripted, content-based lessons that were prepared by textbook companies. Schultz persisted, and figured out how to enact democratic, social justice–oriented, and intellectually rich teaching. What he did, and how he figured out what to do, resonates with the chapters in this book.

Although feelings of cultural shock and disorientation may be more common among White teachers in high-poverty schools that serve mainly students of color, novice teachers of color are not exempt. For example, Hagiwara and Wray (2009) wrote about Nathan, a biracial novice teacher who wanted to work in urban schools, and had some prior successful urban experiences when he was able to use his own Asian cultural background as a bridge for building relationships with students of a similar cultural background. But when placed in an urban school that was culturally different from his background as well as being in a very low socioeconomic community, he found the everyday hard realities of his students' lives to be shocking.

As a new teacher, orienting yourself means confronting your beliefs about what it means to teach and why students respond to school as they do, and your own capacity to form the kinds of relationships with students that will enable you to learn to teach them. Confronting yourself in relationship to your students and the circumstances of your school is essential. In addition, while doing these things, you will also need to be learning the "nuts and bolts" of making your classroom work. Schultz was guided in part by his own experience as a student, in which he had been on the receiving end of high-quality, project-oriented, student-centered teaching, so he was able to visualize what this looks like. However, many novice teachers have less experience with rich pedagogies to draw on, and find it very difficult to resist pressures to adopt "teach to the test" pedagogies that may be expected of them. To help you orient yourself so that your students and their intellectual potential come first, we offer the stories of other teachers' experiences.

In the chapters in Part I of this book, you will journey with two urban teachers as they moved from feeling like complete failures to learning to teach urban students well—and loving it. Both began teaching in schools in which it was accepted as a matter of course that the majority of students would fail. Neither accepted institutionalized failure, but neither began their teaching career knowing how to reverse it.

Eric Mohammed, a secondary social studies teacher in an urban school district, describes the shock he experienced initially in his first teaching assignment, even though he had been the same kind of student as those in his classroom. He then shares lessons he learned during his 12 years of teaching, lessons that focus on how he regards his students and what that regard means for his daily classroom work with them. Rather than offering specific techniques, he offers a way to think about yourself that will enable you to learn and grow as a teacher in your particular situation.

Regina Forni, an English teacher for over 30 years, discusses how her work with students after school prevented her from giving up. Initially, as a seventh- and eighth-grade English teacher in an urban school, she felt like a failure. She tells us how and why she initiated afterschool work, coaching students to prepare them for a public-speaking contest that reached to the state level, and the bonds she formed with students and their parents (as well as other staff members) in the process.

CHAPTER 1

Un/Common Sense for the Prospective Urban Educator

Eric Mohammed

Eric Mohammed is a social studies teacher in a large northeastern school district. He has been teaching for 12 years during which he has taught at several city schools and every New York State social studies course in grades 7–12. Eric also has been an adjunct instructor at the university level.

All through high school, I was a solid D student and proud of it. While others were busy taking notes and answering questions, I was more interested in why my teacher had multiple chalk marks in and around his crotch area, and the inevitable question that followed would lead to my exit from the class. I was very indifferent to studies, and the fact that I had to spend over 40 minutes sitting in a chair was unbearable. I never attended school on a Monday or Friday, those days were reserved for pre- and post-weekend activities. My only thoughts for the future regarded when and how I would procure some weed or a girl, and hopefully, a combination of the two. After 5 years of high school, I finally realized that I had to grow up and make a decision with real-life adult consequences.

After denial letters arrived from colleges, I joined the Army/Army Reserves on a dare from a friend. The military for me was like an extended camp or sleepover with friends, albeit with explosions and heavily armed people. When I returned to civilian life, the only change I could see in myself was that my hair was short, and would remain so, due to my 8-year contract with the Army Reserves. I returned to the familiar rut of inaction and indecision.

In July of 1993, I applied to a nursing program in a small Catholic college near my home, hoping I could use my credentials as a medic in the Army to gain acceptance, but I learned my first valuable lesson: *You cannot escape your past*. The admissions counselor treated my quest as if it were a joke, considering that I had graduated high school at or near the bottom of my class. I went home dejected, but a phone call from a person who identified himself as a minority admissions counselor resulted in my enrollment as an "undeclared" student. I relished the vague sound of it. I felt like an academic free agent, free to explore the world. My sense of freedom was short-lived, however, when I discovered that I would have to attend mandatory tutoring. After one semester, and a 1.7 GPA, I learned another valuable lesson: *Persistence pays off*. It wasn't much, but it was something to build on.

After a few semesters, I was able to see and measure my academic growth. Although I hadn't declared a major, I told my academic advisor that I wanted to "work with people," and so we settled on social work. But after one semester, I returned to my academic advisor, who was my favorite professor—in history, always my strongest subject—and asked him for guidance. What followed was a turning point in life, although at the time it was a simple, short conversation.

The college was an oasis in the middle of a ghetto—a ghetto in which I was born, reared, and lived. As my former 1960s radical professor looked out the window of his sixth-floor office at the city below, he said, "You've come a long way from there, but you still have some more to go. You're like a diamond with rough edges. What do you want to spend the rest of your life doing?" As simple as that question was, I think that was the first time I had been asked to look further than next week. I replied that my strongest area of interest was history. He then asked me how I would support myself with a history degree. My reply was vintage Eric: "Awwww I don't know. How about teaching? That sounds cool, right?" Although I projected a cavalier attitude, I knew that my academic clock was ticking, and I had to make this work. I learned the third lesson in my life: *Be committed*.

I believed that my education coursework would expose the secret life of teachers, and all my questions regarding the profession would be answered. What I found out, however, was that there are no answers when it comes to teaching. I learned plenty of theories, principles, and techniques of my new chosen craft, but one thing kept popping into my head—what if I ever have a student like me? In the weeks prior to my student teaching, I was surrounded by books on lesson planning, classroom management, teacher etiquette, and so on. I went to a local department store and bought my first shirt and tie. The night before I was to begin student teaching I couldn't sleep; I was reciting my lesson plan over and over until it became me. When I arrived 1 hour before the start of school, I was ready to conquer the world. Then something strange happened, and I learned my next life lesson: *Be flexible*.

As a student teacher in a large urban district, I could have been placed at any of the 115 available schools. Although I had no preference, I thought I had a decent chance at being placed at one of several magnet or high-performing schools, as had several of my classmates. I was wrong. My first placement was at Windsor High School, a neighborhood school ringed by public housing projects. After announcing myself as a student teacher, and receiving perplexing looks from the office staff, I anxiously awaited instructions about what I was supposed to do. As the teachers entered the office to sign in, they regarded me with a look that's only reserved for the dead or those about to die. Finally, a smiling face emerged from the mix, and introduced herself as my cooperating teacher.

In the classroom I nervously introduced myself to the students and soon discovered that no one was as excited as me as indicated by the responses to my first request to my new charges—variations on "f – – – that." That's when I realized that my continuing education would take place on my feet in front of kids, not from the sidelines reading theory. The next day, I abandoned the tie and the script, and hit the ground running. I did a decent job running on instinct, and eventually, thanks to the nervous breakdown of another teacher, I was offered his spot a few weeks after concluding my student teaching.

For the next 5 years, everything I needed to know about being a teacher I learned at Windsor High School. I was a pupil of the best teachers I ever had—my students. I knew that I would be successful only if they were successful; we would rise or fall together. We would have each other's back, and to build trust, I had to create an inclusive classroom community where responsibility would be shared and accountability would be enforced. At first, I didn't know how I would do this, but the answers became clear through trial and error.

ON MY OWN: APPLYING LESSONS FROM LIFE

As I look back on my 12-plus years of teaching, I can't point to any specific event or revelation that brought me success or understanding. For the most part, I'm still figuring out this game. By no means do I have the *answer*, nor do I profess any expertise on finding the *answer*, whatever the *answer* may be. As you prepare to enter the classroom, you may feel overwhelmed, anxious, full of self-doubt, and unsure of what you are supposed to do. Welcome to my world. No matter how long you've been teaching, if you feel that you've reached your comfort zone and are totally sure of your ability, you're not doing your job.

What works for one teacher doesn't necessarily work for all teachers. As I said earlier, trial and error can be your best bet. And believe me, err you will. When I was hired midway through the 1998–1999 school year, I walked into complete chaos. I had students hanging out of windows, desks were put into position to form a wrestling ring, half of the class was roaming the halls, and the half that was present could not have cared less about global history. As I surveyed the room, my first thought was, "What did I just agree to?", immediately followed by, "Would it be bad if I quit?"

But quitting wasn't an option for me; I had too much pride. I dug in and decided to make the best of the situation. The first task before me was capturing the students. Literally. I wanted to know my students, and I wanted them to know me. I did 3 days of what we would call openers—student interviews, team-building activities, and so on. We shared our most embarrassing moments, our biggest disappointments, and our goals and dreams. After those few days, we slowly became invested in one another. We started to build trust.

By the end of the year, there was some semblance of a classroom. It wasn't perfect, nor will it ever be, but it was something. When June rolled around, and the students took their exams, I was very hopeful—considering that a few months ago, they were practicing flying-elbow drops from the window sill. After I corrected the exams, my sole thought regarded my future employment. I had a 40% pass rate; I was a failure. I worked for hours after school, I never missed a day, I had tutoring sessions, I did everything imaginable, but it made no difference. Or at least so I thought. When I went to school the next day, I asked to speak with the principal, a man of few words and many scowls. I gave him the results, told him I was sorry, and said I have no problem with resigning, if that's what he desired. After working there for 4 months, I noticed something for the first time—he smiled. "These are the best results we've had in a few years," he said. I was astonished. I disagreed with him and said that the results were terrible, and I'll never forget his reply—"I know they're terrible, but more important, you know they're terrible, and you realize the kids are capable of so much better—you'll do fine next year and beyond as long as you believe in them and yourself."

My first year teaching has become a blur in my memories, but the lessons learned have not. I knew that in addition to theories of classroom instruction, I would need a dose of common sense because you're on your own when the lesson plan fails. Regardless of your situation, you must learn to roll with the punches. So . . . what lessons did I learn from that first year?

LESSON 1: EMBRACE YOUR PAST AND ADJUST YOUR FUTURE

Quite often, we are guilty of imposing our perception of reality on others. We do so without taking into consideration the complex web of historical, social, and political histories of our students. We approach each student from our own perspective, and our own life experiences. A common complaint from students regarding teachers is that they "don't understand us." How do we remedy this? *Develop empathy.* I feel that this is the single most important aspect to building an inclusive community in your classroom. Everything starts with a basic understanding of our students.

Home-life culture will dictate much of the behavior that we will encounter in class. The second "understanding" is that *we can't change this!* Yet empathy will go a long way. Perhaps the key is to infuse home-life culture into the curriculum by incorporating multicultural perspectives and literature on the American experience that mirrors, or brings sense, to what the students have experienced.

Here is an example. In my last year at Windsor, I had the privilege of producing a show for Black History Month. At the time, I was teaching a senior elective called Multicultural Studies, and as a student project, the show fell on the entire class to design, execute, and perform. The students had several skits encompassing history, music, dance, and even comedy. They worked before and after school for 2 straight months. On the big day, the entire student body and parents who attended witnessed a miracle—30 teenagers worked together, without interference from their teacher, and pulled it off without a hitch. They even invited an original member of the Tuskegee Airmen onto the stage during a skit saluting African-American soldiers, and did an excellent job hiding the surprise from me.

The experience I gained from that production was profound. The students relished in the responsibility that was given, and took the initiative to do it right. By actively participating and taking ownership, they truly learned what they taught—and taught everyone else in the process, including me. Don't be afraid to hand over the reins of your class; you may be pleasantly surprised.

The realities faced by many people on a daily basis, both now and throughout history, often conflict with the declaration about "self-evident truths" and "inalienable rights." If anything, students have an inalienable right to know the truth, and to learn of their contributions to our history and experience. Although a full-length school production is great, be mindful that something as simple as a short story or alternative viewpoint for a historical event can spark the interest and engagement of a student. You can't expect students to buy into what you have to say unless they can see how it relates to their own lives.

Although the cornerstone in building an inclusive classroom is empathy, one must be ethical in order to develop that sense of understanding. Far too often, teachers will prejudge students before they enter the classroom. This is not only wrong, and based on assumptions, but it is unethical as a professional to engage in such blatant stereotyping. In my experience, I have found it helpful not to judge a student based on the perspective of another teacher. An assessment of a student should be made by dealing with the student, and in the student's frame of reference. A good talk will get you much further than a disciplinary notice to the principal.

Having similar life experiences to many of my students has always worked to my advantage. However, the ranks of my profession aren't exactly full of people who have shared my perspective. This is where quality urban teacher education is needed. You can't have a classroom community unless you know what that community is about.

LESSON 2: BE COMMITTED, PERSISTENT, AND ACCEPTING

Mutual trust and respect are key to having a successful learning environment. The teacher must provide an avenue of shared responsibility that the students can value. Being committed to students means that a teacher must put temporary feelings of mistrust or uncertainty to the side. Teaching is a transparent profession, and students have the ability to see right through you. If you are not "for real" in their eyes, you're done.

Commitment is key. Offer students several opportunities to build quality relationships with you outside of the role of teacher. In my 12 years of teaching, I have found that the more you invest in the students—whether it is in the form of club advisor, mentor, or just attending a sporting event—the more you get in return from the students. So often, you may be the only adult in their life who takes an interest in them—not as a student, but as a human being whose existence is valid and valued.

As educators, we must be very careful not to judge a book by its cover. The onus is on us to create an atmosphere of acceptance, one in which all students are encouraged, motivated, and prepared to succeed. Unfortunately, we have been witness to instances when our fellow colleagues have referred to students as "these kids," or "these people." I make it a point to immediately correct this error in thinking. They are not "these kids," but *our* kids. Accepting them for who they are and what they can do is a cornerstone in reaching true respect for one another.

A student brings so much more to the class than a brain to be exercised. In my own experience as a social studies teacher, there have been many times when I have capitalized on the identities of my students as "teaching moments." When a Polish American student recalls how his grandfather had to change his name at Ellis Island, or a Somali American student describes the invasion of Mogadishu by U.S. Army Rangers from the Somali perspective, you have to jump at the opportunity. Every student has played a part in the history of our people, and I allow them to share it with the class. Once again, this goes back to validation and voice, the most important factors in self-identity.

Besides what a student brings to class, we must be careful when grading and assessing that we are not criticizing the person, but the work. In addition, we must realize that diverse students may have diverse learning styles, and we must be as accommodating as possible. By allowing students to contribute to their own learning, the community that you build in the classroom isn't just *your* class, but *their* class—acceptance equals ownership, and that ownership equals a shared commitment to success by teachers and students alike.

In 2000, I had the opportunity to be introduced to digital video production in the classroom by way of a university project. The integration and incorporation of film-making validates the often marginalized voice of the student and especially the urban student. As a tool of validation, video production allows students to be both creative and reflective in what they are producing. A student—or any human—wants validation and acceptance. When making a film, unlike writing an essay, a piece of that person is imprinted in the project, and his or her contributions are evident and tangible.

A project like this instills pride in the work produced, and that pride becomes a sense of worth and accomplishment. On a past parent-teacher conference night, I set up a computer for parents to view the work of their children—they were astounded by what their children had achieved. Whether they were the quiet loner type or the class clown, they invested and worked—and now, they're heard. A combination of voice and validation goes a long way in future academic success.

LESSON 3: BE FLEXIBLE IN THOUGHT AND ACTION

We must be aware of who we are, and whom we are teaching. Unfortunately, the current state of urban public education is anything *but* mindful; it is a system designed by and for primarily White, middle-class America. What happens to everyone else? As teachers, we must be cognizant of our style of communication in addition to our teaching methods. Education cannot be approached with a one size fits all mentality. Students from diverse backgrounds require a teacher with a flexible repertoire of effective means of communication. If we cannot communicate effectively, effective teaching is impossible.

Communication is a two-way street—you must have the ability to listen in addition to speaking. There is a tremendous difference between hearing someone, and truly listening. In short, we must be aware that our language should be inclusive of all students—not a select few, or a majority, but all. A condescending attitude will get you nowhere in an urban classroom. We must always be aware in our approach to students, especially in our words and actions. We are role models, whether we like it or not. Our emotions and actions are on display for all to see. We set the tone of the class, and it is up to us as professionals to engage students in the same manner that we would want to be treated.

Unfortunately, not all teachers have this in mind. When I was in fifth grade, I recall my teacher sitting at her desk and telling us that "we would never amount to anything in life; it's not in our blood to succeed." I remember it vividly. Through the course of the year, we, as a class, struggled academically. We were yelled at incessantly, and made to feel so inferior that at one point, no one cared. Eventually, a parent came in to complain. She confronted Ms. Ratchet in the middle of her lesson, and lodged her complaint with a right hook to the face. Ms. Ratchet hit the floor, and the class erupted in loud cheers. It was a surreal experience to say the least.

What can we learn from this? Be peaceful! Ms. Ratchet brought all of her problems on herself. Being combative, insulting students—academically and racially—got her nowhere. As teachers, we must strive for harmony and peace. Above any profession, we must realize that we are all in this together. We pass or fail as a class—not an individual. And it all starts with us.

In addition to communication, flexibility extends into the practical realm of teaching and planning. As you prepare to enter the classroom, be mindful that the best laid plans are subject to total failure, and some of the best instructional moments are unplanned. Be willing to allow a classroom to explore, and encourage and nurture that curiosity. Some of the best teachable moments occur when you least expect them, but roll with it when it happens.

As you and your students explore, you must accept that you don't know everything. And neither do the students. The biggest mistake to avoid is to commit what I refer to as "assumicide." I once worked with a new teacher who was banging her head over the fact that students in 10th grade were unaware of the difference between a continent and a country. I asked her if she taught them the continents, and she replied "No, by 10th grade they should already know that." She was suffering from assumicide. Never assume that all students arrive with a base knowledge. As the teacher operating in class, roll with the punches because it's sink or swim.

When I started teaching, we used chalkboards and ditto machines. Today, I have an interactive whiteboard, projector, and laptop—change is inevitable in this profession, and not just technology. You must embrace change, and lose your fears of letting go of the familiar. So often, we become comfortable with techniques and methodology because it fits us—regardless of whether it works. At times like that, we should remember that we're there for the students, not ourselves. If you do something that works, perfect it; if it doesn't work, assess the reasons why and make improvements accordingly. One of the best words of advice I received came from a veteran teacher with over 30 years of experience who was still at the top of his game—"If you want to stay current, start fresh every year."

Lastly, don't be afraid to approach other teachers and ask to observe them. I learned so much from watching people who have mastered their craft. Observing means nothing if you don't try to implement what works. As I've said before, what works for one teacher may not necessarily work for you, but there is no reason to reinvent the wheel. So many of my classroom practices are an amalgam of those who've come before me. Not everything will work, and you may fail at your attempts—but it's better to fail than fail to try.

CONCLUDING COMMENTS

I have spent the last 12 years of my life dedicated to my profession, constantly striving to do better. In this time, I have encountered obstacles too numerous to detail, but I will say this—it's all worth it. For me, there is nothing more rewarding than touching the life of another, so much so that you have the ability to alter a student's life. It is this aspect that is most humbling, and troubling, at the same time.

As an urban educator, it is so much easier not to care. With such lax oversight and low expectations, our national system of public education encourages incompetence. Furthermore, to invest yourself you must be willing to have your heart broken, and bear a burden that can often be unbearable. There have been times when I reflected on my own experience growing up, and what I've seen in school can take me to places that I didn't want to revisit.

Over the years, I have contemplated quitting, and I'm not ashamed to admit that, either. I have often entertained the thought of opening a coffee shop, and relaxing without a worry in the world. But then, it happens. The thought creeps into my mind as soon as I see myself out of the classroom. What about the kids? Who's going to be there for them? Over the years, I've had numerous opportunities to relocate to the so-called "better" schools, yet I choose the "worst" schools.

I keep at it because someone has to believe that we can get it right, that we can make a difference, and that maybe—just maybe—it will get better. It is this belief that keeps me going on a daily basis. I know that I make a difference, that I fight the good fight, that I honestly try to do something about our current situation in urban public schools rather than complain. I often use an analogy to explain the big picture to my students—"You were born without legs, but expected to run; it's my job to show you the way."

Regardless of the situation, obstacles, and circumstances, failure is not to be accepted. You must learn to overcome, to succeed, to prosper, to obtain the American dream, whatever those dreams may be. I say this because I've learned to run without my legs. And I've been running since the day I was born. If we are to teach students, we must acknowledge that what we are doing requires so much more than what we are giving. If we want change, it starts with us—in our hearts, minds, and within those four walls of the classroom.

CHAPTER 2

Staying After School

Regina Forni

Regina Forni grew up in Brooklyn, New York. After attending several universities around the country, she made her home in western New York. She is a retired secondary English teacher, who taught grades 7–12 in a number of city and suburban schools for 31 years. She has also taught freshman writing and basic study skills in area colleges. During her years of teaching, she was very active in preservice and inservice education, teacher mentoring, and often served as department chair. Her current professional occupations include research coordination, professional development workshops, and substitute teaching. She is also a literacy volunteer, specializing in adult ESL students. She enjoys writing fiction, watching birds, exploring tropical forests, attending theater, and spending cherished time with her children and dogs.

I have always loved to speak, write, and read, so it's easy for me to be very excited about an occupation—teaching secondary English language arts— that focuses on these activities. I'm also crazy about teenagers; I come alive when I'm surrounded by them. So when I first entered the profession, I embarked on classroom teaching with energy, enthusiasm, and hope in abundance, but also, like most teachers, with a colossal naïveté.

My first job was teaching seventh- and eighth-grade English to mostly African American students in an impoverished inner-city setting. The district in which I taught provided well-defined curricula and administered uniform final exams for each secondary subject, grades 7–12. The district also supplied the students with textbooks to learn the curricula and prepare for the final exams. The English language arts curricula and exams were fair enough—for students who were functioning at the seventh- or eighth-grade level. My students, however, were reading and writing well below that. Almost all the instructional materials I was given to work with were beyond them. It was a situation that guaranteed their failure, not to mention mine. Nevertheless, many students passed from year to year because of the district's policy of "social promotion." In the first school in which I taught, only those students who failed all their core subjects were required to repeat courses. The other students were moved up. Students had little incentive to achieve, and by the time most of them got to their secondary courses, they were deplorably weak in English language skills.

I was not ready for this teaching situation. I did what I could to cope, but coping is not teaching. Some days I read simple stories to my students aloud, instructing them to follow along by reading the text. Other days, panicked at how far behind they were, I launched into teaching vocabulary from seventh-grade lists given to me by the district, and I bristled when my students resisted learning words, such as *herald* and *infer*, that made little sense to them. Sometimes we wrote simple sentences; other times I laid out the basics of the five-paragraph essay. There didn't seem to be any in-between kind of instruction. Two other factors made teaching almost intolerable: the behavior of my students, which tended to be wild, impulsive, defiant, and too often violent; and their attendance, which, for too many of them, was poor. Every day was a demoralizing event, for me and for them.

At the end of that first year, two-thirds of my students failed the course, and I decided to resign. My principal tried to talk me out of it. It turned out that a one-third passing rate was "not bad" at that school. Furthermore, he informed me that of the six first-year teachers in the school that academic year, I was the only one who made it past Christmas. This surprised me because I was unaware that there were other beginning teachers in the building. I had spent the year teaching in a dark, anxious bubble. So, despite my principal's pleas, I resolved to leave. I looked back on a year where I felt defeated daily by my job, and I couldn't imagine making a career of it.

After I quit, I spent a summer without a paycheck. I sure did miss that income, so much so that when August was winding down I decided to reapply to teach. It did not occur to me to try a different district. In my eyes, I had failed so completely that no other district could possibly want me. I was rehired by the city and landed in a less stressful school; however, at the end of each day, I found that I was still taking home in my head all that went wrong instead of what went right. That's when I realized that if I were to make a serious go of teaching, I would have to take care of myself as well as my students. The "people" part of education included me as much as it did them. Thank goodness for that epiphany. It kept me from quitting the profession and going to law school.

COACHING FOR A STATEWIDE COMPETITION

To keep myself happy, I resolved to end each of my working days with kids who really wanted to be there; I needed to make the last note of the day a positive one. So I cast about for some afterschool activity that would engage me with interested and responsive students. The district had, and still has, a venerable and high-profile competition for seventh- and eighth-grade students, a public-speaking contest that was established over a hundred years ago with funds from a wealthy benefactor and city dignitary of the 19th century. The students in my classes may have been turned off to reading and writing, but they loved to verbalize. They were not good at formal speaking, but were very enthusiastic talkers, to say the least.

This contest looked like a good opportunity for me to indulge my own passions as well as for my students to show what they could do. And then there was the added benefit to the school. Any student who succeeds in a competition with such an eminent pedigree is bound to get lots of attention, as is the student's school. However, my particular school did not participate in the contest for two reasons. First, no one on the faculty was interested in coaching the students, an extracurricular job that entailed many hours after school with paltry pay. Second, the principal believed that encouraging students to be competitive would destroy any inclination they might have to be cooperative with one another, although his belief did not extend to sports, which were considered a necessary incentive to keep the academically underperforming inner-city kids coming to school. Nonetheless, I approached him with my plan to coach speakers for the contest. I didn't particularly care if I got paid; in my mind, my commitment was a sort of enlightened self-interest. The principal agreed grudgingly. I suspect he thought it would all be a bust anyway—how could public speaking ever compare to basketball? And so in I plunged, with little idea of what I was getting into.

Fortunately, because I taught seventh- and eighth-grade English, I had a bully pulpit from which to recruit speakers. A couple of students signed on right away, but there were a few reluctant others who I thought might do well, and I decided to go after them personally. One of these was a wiry little boy—let's call him Sammy—who was well known in the school for his difficult behavior. He had ADHD and refused to take his medication, so every day he was literally bouncing around the building. He had, however, a lovely big voice, perfect for a public speaker, and I successfully flattered him into competing. Once I had enough competitors on board, I was all set to work with them after school. It was then that I discovered that keeping students after school posed a transportation problem. Unlike the high school students who receive bus passes for 24/7 city transportation, the seventh and eighth graders take school buses back and forth and usually can't afford the city bus fare to stay after school on any regular basis. So I had to get permission from parents to drive the speakers home after every coaching session—something a teacher could do years ago without calling down the law on her head.

My next task was to come up with speeches for the kids to memorize. I really had no clue what would be best, so I turned to rather traditional poetry and literature, just to be on the safe side. My choice for Sammy was "Gunga Din," by Rudyard Kipling. Other students had pieces by Langston Hughes, Tennyson, Poe, and even a junior high version of Beowulf's battle with Grendel. Because my students' reading skills were poor, I recorded their speeches on cassette tapes to make them easy to memorize. Every afternoon, we took over the school auditorium and practiced for 2 to 3 hours. Most of the speakers took direction very well, although Sammy, as expected, proved to be a challenge. I could not get him to assume a relaxed pose when he spoke without inviting endless fidgeting. He also could not manage eye contact with the audience; he'd start laughing immediately. So I made him stand stock-still with his arms locked to his sides and his eyes staring straight ahead, well over the audience's heads and at some imagined vanishing point on the back doors of the hall. In this stance, without moving a muscle, he learned to recite his 5-minute poem.

After every practice day, I drove the kids home. I stuffed them into my little yellow Toyota and went to each of their houses, usually in the poorer parts of the city. I met their families and saw their living conditions. It was an eye-opener for me. The parents tended to be grateful for the attention being given to their children, even though they weren't quite sure what the real value was in reciting a memorized speech. Sammy's parents were supportive but frankly baffled by it all. They probably figured he would flunk out in some way, but they didn't realize that much of the time, his school antics grew out of a determination to be seen and heard. It was my job, as I saw it, to harness that determination and direct it toward something other than getting into trouble.

There are three stages of the contest that speakers face: first, a school-based competition; then, a series of semi-finals, each involving the winners from four or five schools; and then, the all-city final contest. The entire process, from the school auditions and subsequent coaching to the city finals, can stretch out for months. For the school competition, I organized an assembly program with students and teachers as audience. I corralled three teacher-friends from other schools to be the judges, folks who would not be swayed by knowing the speakers in any other context. It was an outstanding experience for all involved. The speakers performed beautifully and became instant celebrities among their peers, while the teachers from my school were treated to displays of talent they didn't know the students possessed. And, of course, Sammy won. I think we were both stunned by the outcome.

It was quite a success for a "bad boy." Unfortunately, the principal did not attend the assembly.

I had known from the start that my coaching would extend beyond the first leg of the city contest. After all, somebody *from* my school had to be a winner *at* my school. But I didn't anticipate spending my afterschool hours for the next several weeks helping Sammy improve his rendition of "Gunga Din." Nevertheless, that's what we did. The semi-final to which we were assigned took place at another school, and the audience for that contest was made up of students and coaches from the participating schools, and members of speakers' families. The kids on the bus that took us there were happy but nervous. First of all, they were not used to field trips, so any chance to get out of the building was an adventure. However, they were unsure what this event would be like, as was I, and how well—or poorly—Sammy would perform. Everybody knew him as a goofy clown, but this occasion called for focus, composure, and self-control—attributes that Sammy was widely acknowledged as lacking.

I can't recall much of the contest, except for the moment when Sammy was pronounced the winner. The kids from my school burst into torrents of cheering and I wondered if I might be dreaming it all. Sammy's parents were delirious with pride. The bus ride back to school was triumphant, and everyone in the school glowed for days. Even the principal, who'd refused to attend the semi-final with us, made a public recognition of Sammy's achievement.

So now we faced the final contest. After many more interminable afternoons of Kipling, we went off to an elegant nonschool location for the auspicious event. Let me begin with the conclusion and tell you that Sammy did not win. He did well, came in third, I think, but he was up against the best of the best, selected from the hundreds of speakers from schools across the city who'd competed just like him. But our principal, interested in seeing what all the fuss was about, broke down and came with us to the final, and had to admit it was quite an accomplishment. All in all, the entire competition was the perfect example of win-win. The principal, the school, and I as the coach came out looking good, while the parents, and, above all, the speakers profited in countless real, although sometimes intangible, ways. Physical poise, mental confidence, and a vision of a positive future are often in short supply among gangly and emotionally eruptive 12- and 13-year-olds. However, that's pretty much what the speakers gained, despite the fact that most of them did not win a contest. As for Sammy, I've run into him a few times since his middle school days, and he's always greeted me with great affection and pride. After high school, he went off to a brief career in the military, and today he has a car dealership in an upscale suburb, where he's no doubt putting those speaking skills to good use.

For the next several years, while I taught at that particular school, the speaking contest was a major affair. Every year, 20 or 30 kids would audition, just for the chance to be coached for the school competition. We wound up having many more speakers competing at the school level in order to accommodate the talent that was showing up. This meant more coaches who, like me, worked with the kids after school without much pay. I collaborated closely with teachers I'd hardly known before and got to meet more and more parents. It also meant a bigger and more celebrated assembly program, during which the students could witness how gifted their peers were. Not a year passed when our school failed to send a speaker to the finals, and our speakers sometimes won first place citywide. During those years, the school's administration changed, as often happens at urban sites, but the new principals were always delighted with the public-speaking reputation of our school and our students. These were ordinary inner-city kids who made everyone proud over and over again. As for me, I was able to develop a deeper bond with the entire school community. Gone were the days when I taught in a bubble.

STARTING OVER IN A NEW SCHOOL

Unfortunately, after a few years, I was transferred to another school. The district ran short of money, there was a giant cutback of employees systemwide, and lots of teachers were shuffled around. I landed in a school that was remarkably like the first place at which I'd taught. The school was run like a prison because no one could imagine doing otherwise. Morale among the faculty was abysmal, and most of the students accepted their lot as academic losers who needed constant supervision. If some felt otherwise, it was because they were unusually bright and looked forward to high school and maybe even college, or they were too belligerent to put up with any attempts at discipline. It was not as chaotic as my first school, but only because it functioned in a sort of permanent lock-down mode. When I broached the subject of the speaking contest, I was informed by the principal that the school did not conduct assemblies of any kind because the students couldn't handle them. Additionally, the doors of the building were padlocked every afternoon 1 hour after the kids left, so practices would have to be curtailed. The teachers were not much more supportive of the idea. I was new to the faculty, so they basically wrote me off as a bit daft, and tended to avoid me.

But I was fired up. The principal did not prohibit my coaching the kids or staging a school competition—he just objected to an assembly program. And there would be fewer speakers to coach, so time after school could be managed. I launched the project the same way I had during that first year at my previous school. And, remarkably enough, nearly the same scenario played out. My "target" recruit this time was a school-phobic girl—I'll call her Paulette—who was repeating seventh grade because she'd simply refused to attend school the year before. Once I'd talked her into competing, she was there every day, if only for the afterschool practices. The school contest was a much more modest affair than I was used to, but we did have an audience and judges. Six or seven speakers did a marvelous job, and, of course, were instantly lionized by the other seventh and eighth graders. Paulette won the school contest and the semi-final, but did not make first place in the final round. However, we looked ahead to the next year, when all the seventh-grade speakers would be eligible to compete again as eighth graders.

Sadly, I was not at the school to help it happen. I was transferred again, this time back to my previous school—a move that I confess I was very happy to make, given the difference in climate. As eighth graders, Paulette and the other speakers approached some of their teachers for coaching, but the best they could get was a teacher who agreed to supervise while the kids coached one another, using the same speeches they had had the previous year. There were no big winners that year, and unfortunately, the school dropped out of the contest. Paulette, however, auditioned for and was accepted to the city's performing arts high school and today is a college grad and a mom. And I was recently contacted by the boy who came in second at that school. He's now a businessman who moonlights as a stand-up comedian. His comedy Web site actually credits the speaking contest as the beginning of it all.

REACHING OUT FROM PERSONAL INTERESTS

Once I'd returned to my former school, the speaking contest again became a staple in my life. I ended up teaching there for a total of 9 years, possibly the most important period of my career. However, I don't know how much credit I can actually take for the years I coached these capable and spirited young people. I was good at what I did, but honestly all they needed was the opportunity, and they were off and running. They weren't prodigies of any kind, just excited and driven the way kids of that age can be. Their success as speakers became everyone's success. And as an added bonus, their sense of possibility spilled over into an enthusiasm for reading and especially for writing. First, they were speaking up a storm, next they were writing one— exactly the way preschoolers develop language skills, or should develop them. In that same school, I started a tutoring program and prepared my seventh- and eighth-grade writers to work with kindergarteners, first, and second graders. Another win-win situation: a validation for my writer-tutors, one-on-one practice for the younger students, and the support and appreciation of faculty and administration. For me, the payoff was what it always had been, a chance to be surrounded by teenagers who are functioning at their best, a chance to bond with them and have their success become mine.

All those years ago what prevented me from giving up as a teacher was finding ways to enjoy myself—my *self*—while enjoying my students. There must be a million ways to do that: music, games, sports, food, religion, the arts, computers, and all the conventional extracurricular activities that most schools provide. Some of these can easily be integrated into classroom teaching. My advice: Start with what you would like to throw yourself into and then invite students to join in. It's easy to shrink the distance between teacher and student when you're both engaged in something you really enjoy. It will probably require more time out of your busy day, but what it adds to your daily routine is invaluable. If your working day consists only of relentless job-related tasks, then you will surely grow to resent it. The main culprit in teacher burnout is *what* you do, not *how much* you do. Additionally, connecting with kids outside of the ordinary school regimen can often contribute to an improvement of their general academic performance. You can even accomplish this simply by going to afterschool sports or musical events and congratulating the kids in class the next day. The point is that when you create rapport with your students, they trust you more, and when you deepen the trust students have for you, you also increase the likelihood that they'll take your word for things, like the value of homework and staying out of trouble. If you can simultaneously help them achieve something that they and others will clearly recognize as success, their confidence in themselves—and in you as their teacher—grows. Knowing that you genuinely care about them can spark a stronger willingness to persevere as students, to work harder and take more risks.

You'll probably also discover, as I did, that there are other folks in the school who share your enthusiasm for whatever you're trying to do with the kids. Sometimes you may be surprised at who's out there. One of the custodians at the last school at which I taught before retiring was also a writer, something I found out quite by accident. I invited him to work informally with my students, and he agreed. For the next 15 years, he was a frequent guest-presenter to my classes and also helped chaperone trips to see local plays. The kids loved it that he worked in the building. They'd seek him out while he was cleaning to talk with him and share their writing. Our community of speakers, readers, and writers was richer because of him.

Community is certainly the operative word, especially when your work with the kids earns the appreciation of their parents. This is perhaps the strongest alliance you can forge as a teacher. Kids are much less likely to do the wrong thing when they know you're on a first-name basis with their moms. Knowing my students' parents also helped me feel closer to the students, less "institutional" in relating to them. I saw the students as part of a family. It sounds awfully corny, but I thrived on that connection. It was something I craved for myself, and the fact that it enhanced what I did as a teacher was almost secondary.

Finally, I'd like to mention administrators. Over the years, I've had more than 10 different principals at the seven schools at which I taught in two different public school districts. I got along with all of them, and every time I departed a school the principal was sad to see me go. That's pretty amazing. I never set out to achieve that kind of record; it just came as a by-product of how I strove to keep myself happy and involved as a professional. For brand-new teachers, pleasing the principal and keeping the job can be a stressful and unavoidable concern. It's not to be taken lightly. Principals themselves are often under the gun, and they may impart their own anxieties about the students and the school to the teachers, sometimes in overbearing and imperious ways.

There are several unpleasant ironies for new teachers, especially those who work in schools where the students' failure to perform has reached crisis proportions. Principals at such schools tend to be very directive, fearing that, if they leave teachers to their own devices, consistency (often mistaken for excellence) will fly out the window. Today, many of the schools in the district where I first taught operate with scripted lessons. Teachers have little or no room to use their own judgment. This may at first seem like the safest option for a principal to take, especially if teachers are inexperienced. But a teacher who can't take a risk is a teacher who is not likely to learn much about what works best for him or her, and new teachers, even in highly successful schools, are often discouraged from taking risks. Another irony is that new teachers, unlike veteran teachers, are given less slack when it comes to making mistakes, despite the fact that they are more likely, simply because they're new, to make those mistakes. A veteran teacher who has established himself or herself as a positive force in a school can get away with a lot more than a new teacher who is just starting out to create a professional reputation. When I stumbled upon the speaking contest, and saw what my students and I could do together, it was quite a eureka experience. No matter where I taught, no matter how unyielding the curriculum or culture of the school, I could always find a way to be productive with kids after school, and usually much more on my own terms. Those afterschool kids were the ones I really fell in love with, even the Sammys among them. So I tried even harder in the classroom to generate the means of their success, and they tried harder, too. Principals like that spiraling good stuff; it reflects well on them. I can recall several instances where my principals were more generous or indulgent with me than with other teachers because they valued what I brought to my job. The good irony for me was that I never set out to keep them happy but to keep *me* happy.

CONCLUDING THOUGHTS

What have I been peddling here? Not so much a way to teach as a way of being a teacher. That "-er" after the word, signifying a "person who does," is essential. We may say that we teach reading or math or science or the piano, but really we're teaching readers, mathematicians, scientists, pianists. The people element simply can't be removed from education, although it can be diminished—and the more it is reduced, the more sterile, unsatisfying, and perhaps even useless the educational endeavor is for everyone involved. The converse is also true: Maximize the people connection, and success, however you may define it as a teacher, is much more probable. Think of the teachers who were really meaningful to you in your life. Chances are they were able to relate to you person-to-person. Maybe it was their sense of humor, or their sincere concern for you, or their drive to share with you their passion for what they taught. Maybe it was their perseverance with your struggles or their patience with your pranks. They probably weren't perfect as teachers, but if the connection they made with you was true and strong, their shortcomings mattered far less.

What I fortunately learned early in the game was that, if I was willing to put some extra time and effort into activities I really enjoyed and if I could get my students to join me, the interpersonal element was guaranteed to grow. And everyone was better off.

PART II

Learning from Your Students

There are many published descriptions of how excellent urban teachers actually learned to teach, and they share a common feature: Teachers needed to learn how to learn from their students. For example, Fred Yeo (1997) described his teacher education program as irrelevant. He "had learned how to construct lesson plans, assertive discipline schedules, different learning styles, and the taxonomy of cognition" (p. 72), but not how to engage urban students, which became painfully obvious when he stepped into the classroom. There, he had to relearn teaching, beginning with learning to listen to his students. As he listened, he gradually figured out how to make use of their interests and knowledge in the classroom, and he began to involve them in making decisions about their learning. Similarly, veteran urban educator Lois Weiner (1999) shared glimpses from her experience. She took a job in New York City, after having had relatively successful experiences as a teacher earlier. She found working in the segregated school of her new job shocking and disorienting; especially vexing was her position as a White person in a largely Black and Latino school in which the students did not trust the predominantly White faculty. It wasn't until she was able to form close personal relationships with students, initially involving them in helping to make decisions about classroom procedures, that urban teaching began to make sense.

We can think of learning to learn from students in terms of a progression. The first critically important step is building a foundation of relationships. Now, this may seem obvious. But the truth is that students who have the most tenuous relationships with school and with teachers—students who are disproportionately of color and/or poor—want teachers to care about them, know them, respect them, and believe in them. (We know this from our own teaching experiences, by the way.) Valenzuela (1999) explained that, based on her interactions with urban students, "youth who maintain that they don't care about school may often really mean something else" (p. 70). For example, she described a girl who had learned to sneer, which served as emotional protection against teachers who made her feel stupid. She actually wanted teachers to care about her, but her experience had taught her that they do not, so she pushed them away.

Relationships, then, become a springboard. Like Lois Weiner did, one can engage the students in helping to solve classroom problems, using a collaborative problem-solving process. Relationships that place the teacher in a position of listener enable him or her to get to know more about the students' lives—what students find meaningful, what problems they are dealing with, what works and does not work for them in school, and so forth. Students will talk if they are being listened to and taken seriously. Based on their interviews with Maori students in New Zealand, Bishop and Berryman (2006) point out that in general, "there have been few attempts to question the assumption that adults, and especially teachers, know more about how young people learn, what they need to do to learn, and how they can learn better than the young people themselves do" (p. 4).

Learning to learn from one's students, ultimately, shifts power relations in the classroom. No longer is the teacher the sole authority, in control at all times. Or, we should say, no longer does the teacher need to work hard to try to retain control. When students have voice—"presence, power, and agency" (Cook-Saither, 2006, p. 363)—and when the teacher listens to them and takes them seriously, that is when successful teachers in real-world schools have been able to build genuine learning communities. Cook-Saither (2006) stresses, however, that doing this "requires letting go of what we think we know and entertaining the possibility of profoundly repositioning students" (p. 381). Similarly, Donnell (2007) describes this process of opening up student voice as "getting to we." She explains that, as teachers learn to listen to their students and build community in the classroom, they no longer see their students "as blank slates or empty vessels, but rather as active agents in their own learning and in the teacher's learning about teaching. Although their pupils were not the only resource for learning about teaching, for the teachers who developed a transformative practice that focused on the exchange between teacher and pupil, they were the primary resource" (p. 225).

In the chapters in Part II, two teachers write about their experience learning to listen to their students. English language arts teacher Frank DiLeo describes what happened when he was assigned to teach an English as a second language (ESL) class in a Buffalo middle school. At first, he "failed miserably," as he put it. When teaching English grammar failed to elicit student engagement, he shifted to taking the students through classical American literature. That didn't work either. It wasn't until he began to use literature the students could relate to that they began to open up in the classroom. Once he began to ask the students questions that related to their lives, then to listen to what they had to say, his approach to teaching underwent transformation.

Elementary teacher Mike Roberts tells stories about learning to listen to his fifth graders' discussions of racism in the context of the social studies curriculum. A White male, Mike tells us about an incident in his own life when he had to reflect on his understanding of racism. That incident sensitized him to his students' points of view when they discussed events in U.S. history and their own lives. Reading his chapter, you will enter into his classroom as he encourages students to say what they think, even when he isn't sure what to do next.

CHAPTER 3

Visionary Teacher/*Maestro Visionario*

Frank DiLeo

Frank DiLeo has worked in the Buffalo (New York) Public Schools for 16 years teaching English at both middle and high schools. His 5 years at the Frank A. Sedita School, PS 38 provided him with invaluable classroom experience. Currently, he is the department chair at City Honors School, a magnet program for the academically gifted and talented students in the city of Buffalo. He teaches courses in advanced placement literature and composition and international baccalaureate literature. Also, he coaches boys' varsity baseball. He lives in the North Buffalo area with his wife, Ann, and two children, Ella and Frankie. His passions are running, cooking, and spending time with his kids.

I am almost sure that I was destined to become a teacher. After all, my mother, after earning her master's degree as a reading specialist, spent 20 years as the principal at St. Margaret's School in North Buffalo, where I attended, graduating in 1980. I then spent 4 years in a college preparatory program at St. Joseph's Collegiate Institute. One teacher in particular left an indelible impression on me mostly because of his way of teaching. He'd walk in to class each morning, his knapsack filled with paperbacks and essays that we had written for homework. We read the classics, Orwell's *Nineteen Eighty Four* (1984) and Kesey's *One Flew Over the Cuckoo's Nest* (1962). In high school I struggled with algebra. My father sat with me nightly, teaching me to find a solution for equations by using the basic rules of simplifying them. So, in my early years, my parents and my high school English teacher were positive forces and models as educators.

In college I decided to pursue journalism. Since I liked to write and travel, I figured that I could make a decent wage and enjoy my work at the same time. During my sophomore year, a professor in the education department came into my literature class to recruit students into the education field. What a fantastic idea! *A teacher—I could change the world!* I saw the classroom as a place where I could teach students to become impassioned with reading great works of literary merit and help them find their voice as writers. In addition, I could enjoy my summers by leisurely reading in the back yard while sipping on iced tea. This image sounded so appealing. Why not?

So I signed up to become a teacher and earned a bachelor's degree in English and secondary education. I settled on a teaching position at Our Lady of Pompeii, a small Catholic school in suburban Buffalo. I would use this opportunity to work on my classroom management skills and to teach creative writing and young adult literature. My original intent was to spend 1 year teaching sixth, seventh, and eighth grades. Although my base salary was a meager $11,800 per year, I really enjoyed working with these kids. Class sizes were small and manageable, and I established a good rapport with the administration and with the Parent Teacher Organization.

After 5 years, I decided to leave teaching to pursue an opportunity to mentor teachers to integrate technology into their daily lesson plans. I believed that learning how to use computers effectively in the classroom would make me more marketable in a rapidly changing technological world. I needed a little luck to land a job in the public school system, so I wanted to be prepared for any opportunity.

BEGINNING AT SEDITA SCHOOL

In the summer of 1998, I received a call from the English language arts supervisor in the city of Buffalo: "Frank, there is a middle school English position available at the Italian school on the west side of Buffalo." *Perfect! I am going back home to teach English*, I thought.

PS 38, or the Frank A. Sedita School (named for the mayor of Buffalo, 1958–1961 and 1966–1973), was a beautiful school located in the heart of Buffalo's West Side. Once the primary home of Buffalo's Italian immigrants, the upper West Side has emerged as an ethnically diverse community. Today, Somali, Sudanese, Middle Eastern, Eastern European, Mexican and Central American, Puerto Rican, and Southeast Asian enclaves populate the neighborhood. Though a neighborhood school, students were also bussed in from other sections of the city. Ninety-two percent of the students qualified for a free lunch. The demographics, according to school records using New York State's categorizations, masked the diversity of the student population: 60% Black, 30% Latino, and 10% White. That particular year, School 77, also located on the West Side, merged with the Sedita School, further diversifying the ethnic makeup of the school. Students attending "multiracial" schools, schools that can either be integrated across racial and class lines or schools that combine three highly impoverished communities of different racial backgrounds, offer both challenges and possibilities. One significant concern at the Sedita School was how to create a positive academic environment with the blending of multilingual, bilingual, and native speakers of Spanish. The solution was instructional leadership, adequate staffing, common planning time for teachers, and equally important a dedicated staff. PS 38 addressed these points.

There is a tendency by the media, movies, and television to stereotype inner-city schools. A typical image of these schools shows overcrowded classrooms with mostly minority populations, unsuitable physical working conditions, and halls flooded with violence and drugs, all leading to a deficient learning environment. This impression hinders the recruitment of high-quality teachers. However, PS 38 was not at all in such shape or characterized by such negative influences. Yes, the students had to struggle a bit more to concentrate, to achieve to the highest of their abilities, but it did not mean that they lacked the ability or means to achieve.

The principal assigned me to room 201, at the northwest corner of the newly renovated part of the building. The classroom connected with three other rooms separated only by an alcove that housed five new G-Macs and empty bookshelves that were begging to be filled with textbooks, paperbacks, and other items that would help establish a home-away-from-home atmosphere. The room had a contemporary feel to it: new rugs, dry-erase boards, walk-in closets for books and coats, air-conditioning, and an office located in the room with a computer.

With only a few days until the start of classes, I needed to make the room functional. I put up a few motivational posters; decorated the bulletin boards, creating a poster with basic rules modeled from the Harry Wong school of classroom management; and arranged the tables in rows, to complete the physical climate of the classroom. I was ready to meet my students.

Day 1: 7:30 A.M. I signed in at the main office and retrieved my class assignments for the semester. I was assigned three eighth-grade English language arts classes, one English as a second language (ESL) class, and one period to monitor the lunchroom. With some trepidation, I told the program coordinator that I did not speak Spanish and had no training in teaching second-language learners.

"You will learn quickly," was her response.

My first-period students slowly filtered into the classroom. After a few general announcements by the principal, I stood in front of the class for the first time. I remember quite clearly: They looked at me, not knowing what the new teacher would say, and I looked at them, not knowing how they would react to the new teacher—it was quiet. I then proceeded to read a poem from a Robert Frost anthology—"Two roads diverged in a yellow wood . . .", the opening lines to "The Road Not Taken." I talked to them about how I was beginning a new journey and how that road I was taking was the one less traveled. I expressed to them that they, too, are that one traveler looking down the road to where it bends in the undergrowth; they are about to take the road less traveled, and that will make all the difference. I waited for applause or some type of positive reaction; instead, they reacted without emotion. I asked them to raise their hands if they had ever heard of Robert Frost.

A boy in the front row raised his hand. "Mister, is he related to Jack Frost?" The other students giggled.

"How many of you read the poem 'The Road Not Taken'?"

"Mister, we don't ever read poetry before."

I articulated in 10 minutes the life and times of Robert Frost. I passed out my expectations for the year and asked them to capture the essence of their summer vacation in 100 words for homework. The bell rang signaling the end of class, and I waited for the next group of kids.

ENCOUNTERING THE CHALLENGES OF AN ESL CLASS

Ten ESL students trickled into the classroom speaking Spanish to one another. When the bell rang to start the class, they continued talking. I desperately tried to get their attention by raising one hand in the air to quiet the class down.

"Power to the people," they shouted and laughed.

Now, my teacher preparation at both the undergraduate and graduate level had equipped me with the necessary skills to develop creative and effective lesson plans. I had thought that effective instruction would be the result of a well-crafted plan. I'd be able to share my love of literature with my students, and they'd listen and produce what was expected of them. However, my education and studying did not prepare me for this particular moment. My idyllic world of teaching was shattered. I'd reached my first significant obstacle as a young White male teacher in the inner city. If my immediate challenge was the language barrier that existed between us, the gulf between my culture and theirs seemed galaxies wide.

For the first few weeks of September, I tried teaching basic grammar, which should play a central role in teaching ESL kids. Yet, the critical question that needed to be answered was, how do I teach the grammar? In other words, how could I help my students learn the grammar they need: Should the basic rules of grammar be presented? Would these grammar lessons help them become better communicators in their own community, a community with which I was only vaguely familiar? I researched articles on teaching syntax and sentence structure, and printed out worksheets for the students to complete in class and at home. The students were uninspired.

So, for the rest of the quarter, I tried to teach works written by American authors such as Hemingway, Steinbeck, Twain, and Hughes. My ESL students were bored, and as a result, I began to feel inadequate in managing the classroom. I struggled with the language; it was an obvious barrier. Not only did the language prove to be a barrier, but certain behaviors that my Latino students exhibited in the classroom were easily misunderstood. We may be living in a globalized world, but the fact remains that there are some subtle—and some not-so-subtle—differences between the expectations that I had for my students and the ones that are a part of the Latino/a culture. For example, in my White Anglo culture, making eye contact shows confidence; failure to look your friend in the eye will not only make him uncomfortable but could be interpreted as a sign that you are being evasive or untruthful. For my Latino students, direct eye contact made them feel uncomfortable. The expectation of eye contact needed to be set aside when my students engaged in dialogue with me.

I also discovered that the word *Latino* groups Spanish-speaking people from various countries who have immigrated to the United States with people who have lived in the United States since the 1600s. Although there is a tendency to lump all Spanish-speaking people together, it is important to understand that Latinos in this country come from many different countries, each with its own culture and history. My ESL students' parents emigrated from Venezuela, Cuba, the Dominican Republic, and Puerto Rico—thus creating a diverse Latino group. So my 11 students were not from one particular culture, but from a variety of origins. Importantly, they identified themselves with their ethnic background.

I spent time with Tandy and Annie, two amazing ESL teachers, who consistently reassured with me that I was a good teacher and that I was doing great things with these students. Yet, there was no gratification. I left the school building daily questioning my ability as a teacher. At night, I worked and reworked my plans, assigned homework—only my students never completed the work.

CONNECTING WITH THE STUDENTS

My lessons failed miserably. I needed to find a way to connect with these kids. Writer Sandra Cisneros said, "It is a great and marvelous thing to be reminded that to change the world we need only to change ourselves" (p. xii in Foreword to Michie, 1999). This became my thesis for change; I researched ESL programs and read about how other White teachers accommodated the needs of their ESL students. By chance, I read *Holler If You Hear Me: The Education of a Teacher and His Students* by Gregory Michie (1999), a book that essentially allowed me to chip away at the metaphoric wall that existed between my students and me. Michie's stories provided me with some insight into how I could connect with my ESL learners. Essentially, I needed to make them feel at home in their school. Michie used Cisneros's *The House on Mango Street* (1991) as a helpful reference for bridging one culture to another and for bringing students' culture into their classroom. I went to a local bookstore and bought Cisneros's book. Cisneros illustrates, through a series of vignettes, life in a Mexican neighborhood, and more importantly, the perception of being an outsider in America. Ironically, I felt like an outsider in the classroom, and my ESL students must have felt alien from the curriculum that I was supposed to teach them. I needed to somehow make learning communal and connect with my students' real world. I hoped to do this through literature from Latino writers.

I bought 10 copies of *Mango Street* for my ESL kids. The next day I gave each student a book and a one-page handout documenting expectations and responsibilities for reading. The brevity of the vignettes would allow us to read aloud in class, which I thought might improve fluency and comprehension. The students kept a journal documenting unfamiliar vocabulary words (this led to teaching dictionary skills) and recording their thoughts, observations, and questions that they might have about characters or plot. I wanted them to react personally to Cisneros's stories, generating discussions, debates, illustrations, and stories from their own families. Since Cisneros's writing had been shaped by her life's experiences, I wanted my students to find their identity and figure out how they fit in with the world around them. More important, I was hoping to help them find their *voice* as writers.

When we began our discussion on the topic of the "American Dream" and what it meant to them, most of my students told how their families left their hometowns because America offered better economic and educational opportunities. I shared how my grandparents left their villages in Sicily with limited resources, hoping to secure a place in America for future generations.

My students talked about their expectations of life in America. "The streets were supposed to be paved with gold," one student, Jose, said squirming in his seat.

"My papa said he needed to find work so that he could send me to college and get a good education," Marya replied.

"People see us as being different from them. Maybe it is because we look different and talk different. It is hard to find our place in the world. I see fancy cars, big homes. You know the stuff you see on TV? How are we supposed to get these things when we don't have money?" asked Tatania.

I said, "That's the dilemma. We need to find happiness in a world where people are judged on what they own. We need to work hard while still maintaining our integrity or character."

Through the eyes of the Cisneros's protagonist and narrator, Esperanza, we read the fleeting events that seemed loosely sewn together about her family and the promise of what the "American Dream" presented to her. However, her epiphany in the end was that her dreams were eroded by the false promises that the "dream" offered her and her family. Perhaps my students and their families shared similar feelings.

Our initial discussions were candid and genuine. *Mango Street* would become a story relevant to my students' lives. As readers, they were forced to think about their own values and relationships in a world that seemed to be different from the one they originally perceived.

ENGAGING THE STUDENTS IN WRITING

I read them a section from the book, titled "My Name." In it, Esperanza, the narrator and protagonist, tells us that her name in English means "hope" and in Spanish means "too many letters." I told them that my name is the second generation of "Franks"; I had inherited it from my grandfather and hoped that someday to continue the tradition by giving my son that name. Since a name has feelings, history, meanings, and memories, I asked them to research their names. Did they inherit their name from a family member? What were the personal experiences tied to their names? How had their names affected them? They began to collect data. Parents, grandparents, and older siblings were interviewed; we held classes in the computer lab where they used the Internet to find great people in history who shared their name. Our classes became more interactive in which the students and I shared writing and reading. Two weeks later, they submitted personal essays and proudly gave 5-minute speeches to their peers on the significance of their names. What impressed me was their passion, their commitment to the task, and their performance.

Another lesson that went particularly well was challenging my students to write a descriptive vignette that illustrated some aspect of their lives, their communities, their cultures. They needed to consider family traditions, heirlooms, colorful characters from the neighborhood, meaningful stories told to them about family members, or anything that made them contemplate their place in their community, in their world. I urged them to model their writing on Cisneros. They wrote their vignettes, creating mental pictures for me by using sensory details, similes, and metaphors to add life to their writing.

Writing is a complex activity linked with cognitive and social relationships. Students write about what they know and have experienced. When my
students wrote about personal experiences, they were given choices about
what to write, thus feeling a greater sense of purpose and ownership.

The challenge for students in any classroom is to move beyond the fear
of talking about race, prejudice, and stereotypes. During the month that we
studied *Mango Street*, race, prejudice, and stereotypes became real issues
that my students discussed in the classroom. Although these are sometimes
viewed as "taboo" topics in the classroom, my students spoke openly about
their own feelings and listened to their peers. Our classroom became a comfortable place where they cooperatively used discussion as vehicle to break
down the superficial barriers that sometimes students may see when they are
isolated individuals. Their willingness to open up inspired the students to
create posters condemning racism, stereotyping, and prejudices. This mul-
tisensory activity forced them to come to terms with their own practices.
They become active advocates for a more tolerant society.

The *Mango Street* experience allowed my 10 ESL students to discover
the beauty and power of both the Spanish and the English languages, uncov-
ering images, words, and sentences that conveyed meaning and emotions.
Considering authorial techniques, rhetorical language, and writer's craft,
we painted pictures from these words in prose, poetry, and art. From this,
I would find my muse as a teacher in the classroom; more important, I inspired and motivated them to be a part of our classroom community.

I spent my prep periods shadowing my ESL kids by sitting in other
classes that they attended during the day. I found it curious that they only
spoke Spanish in these classes. They learned math in Spanish; they studied
the history of the United States in Spanish. They sat together in lunch and
communicated to one another in their native tongue. Yet, for one period a
day, in my class, these 10 students seemed to have a fairly good understanding of English, enough to function in the community around them.

When the *Mango Street* lessons ended, I needed to find other works
for my language learners to embrace as they did Cisneros's work. Wanting
to capitalize on my small successes and keep the kids interested in learning
the language, I consulted my two colleagues, Tandy and Annie. Both had
an incredible wealth of knowledge with second-language acquisition concerns, and were sympathetic, empathetic, and patient regarding the issues of
second-language learning. They became my support system.

During a prep period when I visited with Tandy and Annie in their
classroom, I pulled from the shelf a book of poems by Gary Soto, *Fire in
My Hands* (1990). The illustration on the front cover showed a teenage
girl in the distance and a boy's hand with an orange in it in the forefront. I
thumbed through the book, stopped at a poem called "Oranges," and read
it. Instantly, I thought back to my own teenage years to a time when I first

walked with a girl. I sat down and wrote about that experience. The next day, I read my story to my students. They proceeded to ask questions about the girl: "What happened to her, Mr.?" "Was she good-looking?" "Was she your girlfriend?" For the first time, my reality became their reality. I handed out copies of Soto's poem; I read it to them. I asked them to make connections, as I did when I first read the poem: "Does it remind you of a moment in your life?" "Can we connect this to Esperanza in *Mango Street*?" "Do the characters remind you of any of your friends or older brothers and sisters?" They opened their journals and wrote. At the end of class, they shared some of their anecdotes.

On the ride home from school, I reflected on the activity. I felt good about what happened that day, so I decided to make Soto's poem the focus for the week's lessons. In the poem the boy walks with a girl to a corner drugstore to buy chocolate with a nickel and an orange that he has in his coat pocket. I had the students make a word sketch of the shop as the young kids entered the door. I asked them to use their senses, describing the scene as a novelist might. Then I had the students make a few predictions, particularly about the boy and the girl in the poem. Would their relationship last? Will they have gone their separate ways or will they be married? It is 20 years from now; write something in the voice of the boy or the girl. Again, they wrote. The boys wrote their predictions in the voice of the boy in the poem, while the girls wrote in the voice of the girl. Most of the class predicted that the relationship would end with senior year in high school.

The final activity that I had them work on was to find a line that they thought Gary Soto might have liked and write about all the different meanings the line had for them. In the voice of Soto, I asked them to write a continuation of the line, something the author might have written himself. Again, these lessons became small successes.

THINKING ABOUT A TEACHER'S INFLUENCE

The rest of the school year went well. Of course, some of the challenges continued, but in the end I felt that I was able to connect with my ESL students. They were bright kids and expressed themselves without reservation. I happened to find ways to relate to their lives and to their community without digressing from the state standards. My students listened, my students wrote, my students read, and my students talked. More important, they affirmed an identity.

I am not sure what became of my students from the Sedita School, particularly my second-period ESL students; my hope is that they are living in pursuit of their dreams. Some of them wanted to attend college, while others were content with finishing high school and finding a job in a region that has suffered a decline in population and a surge in unemployment.

As teachers, we want all of our students to be academically successful. Increasingly, the sea of faces that look back at us in the classroom is diverse, challenging us to find culturally relevant ideas to help bridge our worlds. We cannot allow our students to become disconnected from education.

Educators need to continuously reinvent their ideas and adapt to the changing world. We must be ever introspective, and never get too comfortable or complacent about successes. We understand quite personally that educating children in these social and economic times is the ultimate exercise in humility.

At the same time, teaching students is rewarding, although the gratifications are seldom instantaneous. Occasionally, I see former students of mine, and they tell me how much they enjoyed my classes. They remember the personal stories that I told them, the lessons that seemed to resonate with them, and the funny, random quirks that made us laugh together. I cannot recall all those moments, but my students can easily remind me when I see them. I smile and think that I have left an indelible impression on them, much like my teachers and parents did with me. These moments are some of the rewards for our efforts.

"Hey, the Teacher Said He's a Racist"

Mike Roberts

Mike Roberts has been a bilingual teacher in the Salinas, California, area for the past 23 years and has taught all elementary grades from kindergarten through sixth. At the time of writing, his career has reached an interesting point. At the Oasis Charter Public School in Salinas, where his wife of 24 years is the director, his position is half-time kindergarten teacher and half-time custodian. This affords him an opportunity to reach children in a different and challenging way. Mike enjoys gardening, bicycling, offbeat movies, aikido, and reading. He and his wife have two grown children.

Once upon a time, a teacher wanted to teach a lesson about the American Civil War in a sixth-grade class. He had the students open their history books to the chapter that began that era of American history. In reaction to the book's use of a painting depicting the field work on a plantation, one child, Graciela, yelled out, "Hey Mike! That's a racist picture."

"What do you mean?" Mike, the teacher, answered.

"Look at this picture, it's racist!" She shot back, looking smug while using some new vocabulary.

The back and middle ground of the painting were filled with images of Black field slaves. The foreground was dominated by two White figures, probably the owner and his wife. The White man is gesturing in the direction of the field and the many workers in it. "I still don't get it, what's racist? It's what happened." Mike was going to work hard to get the teachable moment out of this. Anticipation of a potential opportunity for off-topic discussion was probably crossing the minds of the more attuned members of the class; Mike was certainly aware that the possibility exists.

"It's got all the White people in front doing nothing, and all the rest are African Americans. They're all like working in the fields and stuff."

Graciela, an English language learner, often relies on the vague language popular among her peers.

"Right, so why's that racist?" Here came Mike's anticipated question.

Graciela asked the devastatingly easy question. "So that's racist, isn't it?"

"I don't think that showing the actual situations and harshness of the conditions is racist, as long as they try to keep the painting as honest or real as possible. They are showing a racist situation, but that doesn't make the painting itself racist. It shows something that was horribly racist." Mike was sure that he's really a great teacher and had done something remarkable. At least he exposed Graciela to some of the fine points of the English language and its uses.

Now Nelida chimed in, "Isn't that just like here in Salinas? In the fields the workers are all brown and the bosses are White. White people don't work in the fields picking stuff!" Her eyes lit up; she loved these discussions.

This is not going where Mike wanted it to go; there are so many more social studies standards to cover and this is just the beginning of the Civil War unit.

It's my own fault (yeah, I'm Mike) that I got to this point. I didn't really set out to have the students address race and its implications in our history. One can rarely control children's spontaneous reactions.

Perhaps, this is a good place to describe something of my journey from being a working-class kid in a (particularly) racist community to becoming a teacher encouraging his students to have heart-felt and passionate conversations about racism in their classroom.

PART OF THE PROBLEM OR PART OF THE SOLUTION?

As a White middle-class male, I often question my role in the process of discussing racism in the classroom. Why me? Shouldn't my students be asking these questions of someone closer to them? Isn't there someone better qualified to do this? I've never studied racial identity, or how to handle the questions asked by the students.

All I have is an honest nature, an ability not to take this too personally, and a good vocabulary. As a teacher, one has the responsibility to allow children the chance to express their thoughts and observations of the world around them. Since most standards want to foster the development of orally expressive students, discussion becomes part of the teaching/learning process. In a society like ours, where race is such an important issue, I probably have spent more time than the average middle-class White guy thinking about the effects of race and racism on my teaching and my students. In addition, I think it's important that my students feel that there is a safe atmosphere in our classroom. Almost any question is fair game, if asked appropriately, and/or at the proper time and place. Maybe this is enough.

Just as we would do with reading, math, and science (especially science), it is simply good teaching to bring personal experience into a classroom. To me, it seems imperative to make sure that all the children have an opportunity to talk about their experiences, interpretations, and assumptions. How else are children going to take the rest of my teaching seriously if I don't allow them to speak about their basic identity? How do I reveal to them that I, like almost everyone, have some prejudices and biases? That I, too, have been racist at times?

As a White person who has lived in bigoted communities, I have often been faced with remarks and attitudes that reflect the opinions of the speaker's milieu. At parties, in informal conversations, and at times even in staff meetings, people say the stupidest things. I have dismissed their remarks with a simple remark, "Well, you know that's not really true for all."

Directly addressing the person's racist remarks is one way to feel as if I have done something, and I have made myself feel better by saying something. However, was that the best way to do something about it? After much reflection and exposure to several people who have thought much on this issue, such as reading books by William Ryan (1976), Lisa Delpit (1995), and Louise Derman-Sparks and the Anti-Bias Task Force at Pacific Oaks College (1989), and conversing with Christine Sleeter and Louise Derman-Sparks, I came to realize that my path was to help children come to terms with the attitudes and forms of institutional racism they will face, and to provide a place where they can talk about what they hear, see, and feel.

When students have spoken up about an incident or I, as their teacher, have witnessed something ugly, it isn't enough to say, "Yes, you're right, that is a stupid thing to do (or say). That's mean, and we don't do it in our class. Now let's review your homework." People, particularly children, need an opportunity to process their experiences. We need to remember that children are just beginning to develop their schema in many areas of their lives. When they observe something out of the ordinary, or outside of the boundaries of their idea of fairness, they require an opportunity to think about it and ask questions of a trusted person, whether the incident occurs on the playground or in the so-called real world. Remember, though, that the playground *is* a part of their real world.

Children come to us aware of the differences in their size, attractiveness, and skin color. They have internalized these notions. Over the years, I have noticed that the pretty children cluster together, the active ones chase each other about, and all children look for others who look like themselves. Children also try to engage the attention of the more popular individuals. Many of us have heard and seen children teased by other students for the color of their skin or the way they talk. Like other teachers, I have been forced to find ways to address these issues, although I have never felt totally qualified. Reading and conversations didn't give me the grounding I thought necessary for dealing with such serious issues.

I think, though, a story or two will provide some insight into how personal experiences have affected my point of view about racism. Please be patient with me while I give a quick tour of some of the events in my life that started my journey down this road.

IF NOT YOU, WHO?

Before I was a teacher, I cooked in various restaurants in Chicago. Several of them were owned by a large company that had restaurants in different locations throughout the Loop in Chicago. I was filling in at some of these on a rotating basis. On one occasion, I had been given particular instructions from the general manager on an unusual customer request to be filled the next morning. The woman who normally handled the morning operations was an older African American and had worked for the company much longer than I had.

I told her of the request and how management wanted it handled. "We don't do that," was her reply. I said that I didn't know, but that's what I'd been told. We went back and forth like this several more times. I think she was resentful of my imposed role and wondered (to herself) just what that was going to be in her restaurant, during her shift. She ended the conversation abruptly with, "Well, if you're White, you're right!"

I was left with nothing to say. "I . . ." tumbled out of my mouth. I walked away very hurt and confused. I hadn't pulled rank or anything like that on her. I had just told her what I'd been told. What I wasn't aware of was her history and what that had taught her. My first real lesson in White privilege had been delivered. Before that, obviously, I knew things about the world: that I was White, that it was easier for me to get interviews with prospective employers, and that there were people who assumed things about me because of my color. The angry and personal nature of her reaction and the history behind that statement has stuck with me ever since, a pebble in my shoe, so to speak.

My first position as a teacher was working in a bilingual fourth-grade classroom in a rural farming community; all but three of my students were Latino/a, with widely varying degrees of English capability. One of the highlights of fourth grade in California is visiting the old missions in order to enhance the social studies curriculum. Luckily, there are several excellent examples of restored missions in our area. The first choice of many is a mission renowned for the beauty of its restoration and its gardens. It is something of a tourist trap.

I had arranged a field trip to this mission and had done all the many activities getting the children interested and knowledgeable about the mission era. Knowing that there are beautiful flowers at this site, I also did some extensive science lessons about flowers' reproduction and the importance of their appearance. My students were ready for their first mission experience.

Their enthusiasm and excitement were indeed at a high level. There were many learning opportunities available at this example of California's rich history. Unfortunately, I had not prepared the students for the attitudes and prejudice they would meet in the gift shop and gardens. The reaction of the gardener was reported to me later by one of the students, Jose Luis, as, "Get the f*** away from the flowers." I personally overheard the parish priest say in sotto voce, "Well, if they don't know how to act, they won't be invited back." (Yes, this is an operating church.) A group of girls also reported later that the women in the gift shop kept asking them if they were going to buy something or not, then asking the students to leave if they weren't going to buy. It appeared to me that the attitude of the padres—that the natives are backward heathens—has not changed much in the 200-plus years since the construction of the missions.

Upon our return to the school, the subsequent conversation about the experiences at the mission revealed the universality of the bigoted and prejudiced reception we received there. I had had no idea that the gardener had spoken so rudely to the children, nor about the attitude of the gift shop clerks. The students were unhappy about the experience and felt they had done nothing to warrant this treatment.

I will be the first one to admit that this was a loud and energetic group of students. They had an inexperienced teacher leading them, and this was only my second big field trip with them. Most of them had marveled at things like escalators and elevators, even climbing staircases on the previous field trip. You can imagine the effect that the majesty and beauty of an old church might have upon them.

By way of comparison, I saw another school group at the mission that day. A friend of mine was part of that group, chaperoning his daughter's class. He noted later that his group had been as noisy and excited as ours. They, however, had received no vulgar admonitions from the gardener, no comments from the priest, and no rudeness in the gift shop. They, as you might guess, were from a well-to-do community and were predominantly White.

During a later conversation with the class I mentioned this and again received the full fury of their ire. "Why were those people like that?" "We were going to buy stuff." "I was just looking at the flowers!" "They just don't like us because we're Mexicans." These were among the angry responses they flung at me. What to do?

Again, the teachable moment arose. "Let's write them a letter and explain our point of view." The class loved this idea. We got to work; drafts were made and edited. (I have to admit that this frenzy of focused activity spoiled me for students' later reluctance to edit and rewrite on other, more mundane, topics.)

We finally came up with a letter the class could live with. It was error-free and to the point. We sent it off with feelings of hope and wounded self-righteousness. We waited weeks for the reply that never came.

You would have to ask the personnel at the mission why they never responded to our letter. I can say that the experience led a group of young children to feel that there is no reason to believe that people will apologize for or even recognize their racist behavior. Taking them seriously and allowing them to express their frustrations in an appropriate way somehow seemed the best thing to do, although it ultimately proved inadequate. For me and for all of my students, I'm sure that we did the right thing.

AND NOW WHAT . . . ?

These two incidents along with more than a few others have convinced me that my situation in life has benefited me enormously. They have also mandated that I advocate for those not in my position. Anyone considering teaching as a profession has to think about the issue of race in their school community. From protesting that non-English-speaking children shouldn't be given a standardized test in English (a political act) to comforting a child and aiding her in expressing her feelings about playground taunts (a humane act), every teacher has an opportunity to help, advocate, and work against the daily grind of racist attitudes and systems. I, for one, am not a special person with a unique set of skills or personality geared to advocating.

As I mentioned above, I was raised in a racist community. It hasn't been easy to look at my personal actions and reactions. When I admitted to my class that I am a racist, one student, Gerardo, couldn't hold in his eagerness to pelt me with questions. "Who are you racist against?" "Why do you hate them?" Gerardo is highly attuned to this topic. This year, he is the one who will not let go of the issue. His questions have much to do with power, its use, and who has it.

I think, though, that I need to back up a little bit here to provide a bit of context.

In Salinas we have a terrible gang problem. In the past 2 and a half years more than 60 young people have been killed in gang-related shootings, some of them innocent bystanders. For years before this, schools had been acting in a variety of ways toward gangs, from banning gang-affiliated clothing, to adopting uniforms and attempting to inform parents and teachers about the signs to watch out for. To my knowledge, none of the schools or their districts has actually asked the kids what they think.

Gerardo is part of an extended family that is affiliated with one of the two major gang groups involved in this bloodbath. He dresses and asserts himself in a "gangbanger" way. He really wants to get in a big conversation about "La Vida Loca." As a result, anything that I say about Mexicans, gangs, the colors red and blue, or race can easily get Gerardo going, so much so that the other students often groan when he brings up a topic in a class meeting. As an example, in a class meeting he asserted, "Mike insulted Mexicans when he said that most of the gangs in Salinas are made up of Mexicans." Then the class awaited my response, and we were off to a lively conversation filled with misunderstandings, clarifications, and heartfelt assertions.

My response in this case was basically that the names of the murdered I see in the media and the people (very few) arrested by the police for the murders are of Hispanic background. This was understood by another student as, "All Mexicans are gang members." As a result, I said something to the effect of, "Well, I didn't say that; I'm not that stupid and I'm not that racist."

"So you are racist, you admit it. Who are you racist against? Why do you hate them?" Gerardo questioned me assertively.

Without admitting anything in particular, I answered that I was raised in a racist community and the attitudes can be hard to get rid of, that all of us have some things that stay with us. At this point, I am at the very edge of my personal understanding of this issue.

This is a scary place for a teacher to be. Where am I going with this lesson? What the hell have I gotten myself into?

Luckily, another student chimed in, saying that there are other types of gangs and that they could be doing the shooting. This led to a discussion of the ethnic makeup of our city and the likelihood of our violence being the result of African American, Japanese, Chinese, or Italian gangs—none of which is likely given the facts of our demographics. Reality has never stopped children's imaginations, thank goodness.

The larger question still looms: "How do I address Gerardo's question?" How does one address the complexity of racial relations in the United States? Is it even possible to explain to an 11-year-old in the context of our classroom?

THIS IS WHAT I DO

I hope that these questions are causing a lot of disequilibrium in your mind right now. You might never have to deal with these and other complex questions in your career. There are many places to teach and many children with many challenges. The aspect of teaching that makes it different from other careers is simple.

As teachers, who we are is as important as what we teach. My experience in cooking showed me that any technically qualified person can cook food. There are better and worse cooks, but we aren't too much concerned, for instance, with the cook's racial attitudes. But as a teacher, the person you are as well as your beliefs are important. We are not just slapping burgers on the grill, or attaching widgets to a gizmo.

The person standing in front of that group, and his or her background, beliefs, and understanding, are of utmost importance to the students. Certainly, all of us have had experiences with a broad spectrum of teachers. Those we had at younger ages probably inspired our career choices and are the reason you're reading this now. That person made you want to be a teacher. A teacher with unspoken racist attitudes can perpetuate much hate in our world. Don't for a moment pretend that there aren't any out there. Anyone with any time in our educational system will verify that there are more than you might imagine.

How do we get children to be comfortable enough and able to speak their minds? In my school, I have the privilege and responsibility of working with my students for more than 1 year. We are also a small school, and the students know all the teachers, having been in their classrooms many times for one reason or another. As a result, the majority of students in my class have known me for quite a while. The level of trust is very high.

In a typical public school, working with the same students for more than 1 year is unlikely. But there are other ways to create relationships with other, younger students. Seize any excuse for a cross-grade activity involving younger students. (We all know this is impossible for kindergarten teachers, unless your school has a preschool attached.) Eventually, these will be your students—maybe not all of them, but enough to start with.

On the playground, during yard duty, during crossing-guard duties, and so forth, engage the students in discussing their games or media-related clothing. At the moment, Hannah Montana/Miley Cyrus and skater looks dominate, but TV shows, clothing logos, and so on all can generate a comment or a joke. Personally, I get to act completely clueless and ask lots of questions because, obviously, I know nothing, given my grandfatherly appearance. That option is not available to all. However, we all have things we can do and can share with kids. It's okay, in most schools, to hit the tetherball a few times or pass a ball during yard duty, but please don't talk just to the really nice girls who want to be teachers! They need attention, too, but they are the ones who almost always get a lot of it.

After school, there are often kids in a neighborhood school who hang around, not really wanting to go home yet. Put them to work, if you are allowed to, or try it and find out that you aren't. Start an afterschool club.

Kids will talk during these times more openly because it's not "school." As one opens up a discussion on a topic, it might go anywhere. This is never truer than with elementary schoolchildren who have been allowed the opportunity to openly address topics that affect them deeply. They are likely to bring up anything that is on their minds.

In one's own classroom, the process takes many forms. At the heart of it, the students must care about one another's opinions. Professionally, I learned to use class meetings, which have worked very well for my classrooms for many years. Over the years, there have been some traditions: an object to pass—students must get up and hand the object to the person they are talking to (or about); silliness—using the class meeting to tell a joke or bring up an obviously resolved issue just for a laugh. Some individuals never seemed to learn to respect the opinions of others or the rules and are regularly asked to leave the meeting. The axiom "there's one in every crowd" is also true in classrooms.

The rules, unwritten and written, of our class meetings are well established; scapegoating is not permitted, courtesy is required, the group's opinions are always solicited. When the students are asking serious questions of one another or the teacher about policies and rules, it is obvious that they are comfortable. I finally was made aware of the degree of comfort when Lorena announced, "I have a problem with Mike." The class let out a collective gasp. It was small but obvious, like a fly circling the room. From there, the level of trust and confidence grew until even a new, shy student could come up with her own problem with me.

I want to make sure that it is understood that I listen seriously, apologize when appropriate, and explain my decision(s). I do not always change policy, or even apologize for a consequence administered to an offended and protesting student. The point of this is to let the students know that someone is listening empathetically to their complaints and will, when appropriate, help them take action on their concerns.

The class meeting is an ideal place to begin a process toward building more trust. There are many books on this topic, and I can't really identify the model I use, but the process is the important part. Find a structure that suits you and use it. Then change it to suit your personality, remembering that you will be using this for a while and you'd better like it.

Once that trust is established and the students can voice their concerns and opinions, then the classroom takes on a different, more comfortable feeling. Students start visiting one another's homes, and sleepovers start to occur. I have found that when students share what they did over the weekend, other class members are part of the story. Two or more students have the same story because they did the activity together. Or, one could argue that the trust comes as a result of the friendships begun outside of school. Either way, the starting point of trust is in the classroom; that is where the initial contact happens and sets the stage for the relationships that bind the group together.

A CUMULATIVE EFFECT

Graciela and Nelida have been left hanging and courtesy requires that we address them before we part ways.

With all his knowledge of social class, labor struggle, and civil rights, and with a United Farm Workers flag on a shelf in a cupboard, Mike tried to explain that the work, as most of the students know, is very difficult and grueling. People who have other options don't go into field work. People who do go into it often try to find a way to move into other positions, usually related to field work or agriculture. Certainly, the people working in the fields don't want their children doing the same backbreaking work. Most frequently, the parents want their kids to know how hard field work is in order to motivate them to work hard in school and have other options. Many of the kids have seen first-hand the racial relations in the fields around Salinas. As a result of seeing the world as it is around them and feeling as if they can ask almost any question they have in mind, my students formulate uncomfortable questions. The underlying question is, "How does this social/economic arrangement affect me in my life?" Or, "Why do White people have almost all of the good jobs in the big businesses in Salinas? Why does it always seem to be the newest, darkest, and least powerful who end up doing the most difficult jobs? Why doesn't my mom/dad get a chance at better positions?" I hope by the time they are in high school they have asked many other questions about the distribution of wealth and power in their society.

Since the students likely have more experience than I do in dealing with the personal aspect of Salinas' racial relations, I'm going to turn the problem back over to them. "Why do you think that the fields are owned by White people and the workers are brown? What is the history of our community in dealing with this problem? Is it only brown people who have worked this hard for so little money in the fields?" This is where the curriculum bursts the classroom walls and spills into the real world.

It would be gratifying to present the splendid results of our class's efforts to erase racism. However, that is not how this story ended. Nelida's interest has continued; she wrote an interesting and challenging report on Tookie Williams, the founder of the Crips who went on to reform his life in prison. Other students continued the conversation in their own idiosyncratic ways. Gerardo kept throwing odd questions, like bombs, to the adults in his life. Since the school is small, I am able to keep in contact even though I recently changed grades to teach early primary.

The problems of Salinas and the United States and the world are not solved by my interactions with my students in our classroom. My hope is in the ripple effect of one student asking the right questions in the right circumstance and awakening the minds of her peers. Then they start to ask questions and attitudes are changed. Changes in attitude can then become action. In our community, there are more Latino/a municipal and county leaders than ever, because someone asked, "Why not one of us?" So, the question then becomes: Why not you? What is the role you can take in dismantling institutional racism? Because it's there; all you need to do is look.

PART III

Thinking Creatively About Curriculum and Pedagogy

New teachers face what often feels like a contradictory task: trying to engage students in high-quality learning, and using a standardized curriculum that may be backed up by an officially sanctioned standardized approach to teaching and standardized statewide exams. If you are teaching in a school that has a history of doing well on tests, you may be given a fair amount of latitude in how and what you teach, as long as you are addressing the state standards. But if you are teaching in a school that has not tested well, your work may be much more tightly controlled.

Popular belief holds that if teachers stick to a curriculum that is closely aligned with the state's tests, students will learn better. Ogawa, Sandholtz, Martinez-Flores, and Scribner (2003) point out that, from the point of view of administrators, having clear goals should reasonably help teachers coordinate their teaching, which should, in turn, improve student academic achievement. But this logic is applied widely in ways that contradict much of what is known about student learning. For example, Ogawa and his colleagues found that the administrators in their study invested considerable time, energy, and resources shaping how specific standards should guide teaching, purchasing materials that are standards-aligned, and getting teachers to buy into the system. At the classroom level, however, there was no shared philosophy of good instruction. As a result, discussions of standards-based curriculum dominated without consideration of good teaching, and the teacher-centered delivery of standards-based content prevailed. Student interests and prior knowledge were ignored in the process, as was use of instructional strategies that engage students actively.

This is a widespread problem. Au (2007) synthesized findings of 49 studies that examined the impact of high-stakes testing on curriculum and/or instruction in U.S. schools. A majority of the studies found that the response to testing was to narrow curriculum so that it would align with tests. Almost half of the studies also found curriculum to become more fragmented rather than coherent as teachers worked to make sure the tested content would be taught; in only one-fifth of the studies did teachers integrate the curriculum around meaningful ideas. Two-thirds of the studies found that pedagogy became more teacher-centered; only a handful found teaching to become more student-centered.

In the introduction to this book, we examined the value of culturally relevant and intellectually engaging teaching. Although the relevance
of curricular content matters to students in terms of their willingness to
engage with it and their subsequent learning, cultural relevance is often
not considered in standards-based reform. And although intuitively one
would think that an intellectually engaging approach to teaching would
improve student learning, adherence to standards can push in the opposite
direction—against intellectual engagement. For example, in an analysis of
the California state standards, Manthey (2006) found that "just over one
quarter of the standards are written at a 'remember' or an 'understand'
level," while only about 5% are written at a "create" level of thinking.
Strict adherence to standards, in this case, would push away from, rather
than toward, intellectual engagement.

Further, student-centered teaching processes, supported by a sizeable
body of research, very often simply go by the wayside. Cooperative learning, for example, has a strong and consistent track record of improving student learning, when used appropriately (e.g., Cohen & Lotan, 1997; Nastasi & Clements, 1991). About 15 years ago, the American Psychological
Association established a set of Learner-Centered Psychological Principles,
based on a synthesis of research on conditions that best support high levels
of achievement. According to McCombs (2003):

> Putting learners first is at the heart of learner-centered teaching. The focus is
> shifted from "what teachers teach" to "what students learn." Learner-centered
> teachers understand that they must find ways to know their individual students
> and provide a safe and nurturing context before the job of teaching can begin.
> Learner-centered teachers also understand that not only is learning a natural
> lifelong process, but motivation to learn also comes naturally when the learning
> context is supportive. (p. 96)

Learner-centered teaching is based on teachers getting to know their students, as illustrated in Part II of this book. But ironically, rather than being
expected to focus on student learning, teachers are very often directed to
focus on what content they deliver instead.

The challenge for new teachers, then, is figuring out how to teach to the
expected standards, but in a way that is flexible with curriculum content,
responsive to students, intellectually rich, and uses engaging pedagogical
strategies. Ideally, new teachers would not have to figure out how to do
this by themselves, but would be collaborating with more experienced colleagues. But "real-world" contexts are frequently distant from that ideal.
How, then, have individual teachers managed to navigate this challenge successfully in less than ideal settings?

In the chapters in Part III, three teachers share their experiences learning to work creatively with curriculum and pedagogy, so that their students not only develop interest in academic learning, but also do well. Veteran teacher Katharine Richman shares a unit about agriculture that she teaches her first-grade bilingual students. When curriculum reform shifted to standards-based reform in the late 1990s, she struggled to retain the student-centered, culturally relevant approaches to teaching that she had learned how to use. In her chapter, she shares with new teachers how to plan a rich thematic unit and map it against the curriculum standards they are expected to follow.

Juanita Perea describes challenges she faced as a second-grade bilingual teacher. Initially, she had considerable freedom to plan curriculum that responded to her students. However, when her district adopted a curriculum package that everyone was expected to follow, she found that freedom quickly eroded. Her chapter tells us how she learned to creatively uphold high academic expectations in a learner-centered classroom, while resisting institutionalized pressures such as pacing guides.

High school math teacher Stephen Stiller shows how and why he created a method of teaching that hooks inner-city students. It is based on a shift from viewing students in terms of "they can't" to "they can," from lecturing at students to working with them. His method makes excellent use of principles of student-centered teaching and cooperative learning. Even students who initially regard math with complete disinterest, and students who usually cause trouble in the classroom, become hooked on math in his classroom.

CHAPTER 5

Teaching Thematically
in a Standards Context

Katharine Richman

Katharine Richman was born in Nayarit, Mexico, and grew up on a family farm in southern Ohio. Her parents were high school teachers. She spent time in Mexico as a child and later lived there for 3 and a half years after college. She has been teaching for 30 years, kindergarten through third grade, and at present teaches first grade in Salinas, California. She loves sharing literature, music, and the great outdoors with children, as well as traveling, hiking, and quilting.

During the past 10 years, it has become more and more difficult to be creative and student-centered. We classroom teachers are usually required to teach from a prescribed, state-adopted curriculum. The No Child Left Behind Act has had the effect of emphasizing language arts and math at the expense of all other areas of study in the elementary and middle school grades. In an attempt to raise test scores, administrators and school boards often try to limit what materials may be used to teach and decree exactly how many minutes should be spent on each curricular area. It can be a daunting prospect to try to depart from what is expected, but it is possible to teach an integrated thematic unit while still following grade-level standards and supplementing the required basal texts rather than replacing them completely with one's own materials. In this chapter, I'll be talking about how to develop a thematic unit that fits your grade-level expectations and will challenge and interest your students, yet will be acceptable to administrators.

First, let me give you a little background about the students I teach and about myself as a teacher. Every year in August, I feel a sense of anticipation and suspense. I am about to be given 20 surprise packages, which I will help to open over the course of a school year. Who knows what these 20 students will look like and how they will change during a year in my classroom?

My 30 years of teaching have sometimes been grueling, sometimes exasperating, sometimes celebratory, sometimes transcendent. Teaching has rarely been boring. If we remember that we are teaching students rather than covering material, we retain the ability to be surprised, thrilled, satisfied, and humbled by our students and the joint enterprise we call school.

I teach in a K–6 school in a mid-size California city surrounded by fields of lettuce, broccoli, strawberries, and artichokes. A bilingual teacher, I have taught only one student for whom English was a first language during the past 15 years. Some of my students were born in the United States, others in Mexico. At the beginning of a typical school year in first grade, a few of my students can read fluently in Spanish. A few others may know some letters but may be unable to read or write anything except their names. The remaining students fall somewhere in between. All are working on learning English as they become literate in their first language.

During the course of the year, I try to develop in my students a hunger for literature by reading them many books, picture books in English and Spanish and chapter books in Spanish. I try to awaken their interest in the world around them and help them make sense of it as we discuss the school, the community, and our country as well as others. Together, we work to create a sense of community in the classroom, partly through the use of class meetings and conflict resolution. Parents are welcome to spend time in the classroom—many stay for the first 15 minutes of the day to read with their children. Some parents volunteer in the classroom, particularly during the months of November to March, when the fields lie fallow and many are out of work.

WHY I CHOSE TO DEVELOP A UNIT ABOUT AGRICULTURE

I teach in an area where agriculture is the lifeblood of the community. California produces a high percentage of the country's fresh fruits and vegetables. Much of this produce is raised on huge "factory farms" owned by large agribusiness corporations. Yet, some people have found alternative ways of raising food that do not rely on genetically modified seeds or on harmful chemicals. The conflict between what agriculture has become in this country and what it can be is the reason I chose to develop a unit on agriculture. Most of my students' parents work in agriculture, yet very few can aspire to being farmers.

I grew up on a farm in Ohio that my mother's great-great-great-grand-parents began farming in 1810. When my mother was growing up, her family had a dairy, chickens, a few sheep and hogs, crops of corn and some tobacco, and enough fruit and vegetables for their own use. In the late 1950s, my uncle decided that he could no longer make a living farming that land, and no one has tried to make a living exclusively from the farm since then. I haven't lived on the farm for 30 years, but I still feel a strong love for that land. Most of my students' families come from rural areas of Mexico where their families farmed the few acres they had; many of them came to this country because they could not survive on the land they owned. The situations are not comparable, but the attachment to the land, to taking care of it and being stewards of it, is something with which I identify. In California, large corporate farming has been the norm for many years. Due in large part to government agricultural support policies, this has become true for much of the rest of the country as well. I want my students to understand the importance of agriculture and that there are alternatives to the agribusiness model of farming. As Wendell Berry (1977) wrote,

> I conceive a strip miner to be a model exploiter, and as a model nurturer I take the old-fashioned idea or ideal of a farmer. The exploiter is a specialist, an expert; the nurturer is not. The standard of the exploiter is efficiency; the standard of the nurturer is care. The exploiter's goal is money, profit; the nurturer's goal is health—his land's health, his own, his family's, his community's, his country's. (p. 7)

Certainly, not everything my class studies during the school year is related to agriculture, but I have been able to develop activities in language arts, mathematics, science, and social studies that relate to different aspects of agriculture and address grade-level standards in the various curricular areas. In this chapter, I will discuss how I went about developing my agriculture unit and how it would be possible to adapt such a thematic unit to the needs of different grade levels.

CHOOSING A THEME

As you think about selecting a topic for a unit, keep in mind that a theme should be something in which you yourself are interested. Doing the work required to develop a theme will be rewarding only if it deepens your knowledge and your students' understanding of something that you really care about. Don't choose a topic just because it is "covered" by your grade-level curriculum if you have no interest in the subject. It is helpful to read material that develops your background knowledge of the subject in addition to material that you can use with your students.

When you are choosing a theme, make sure that it is both broad enough and substantive enough to allow for creating a range of related activities that span many areas of the curriculum. Although it might be tempting, particularly in the lower grades, to choose "fun" themes such as apples, fish, or teddy bears, these topics have limited possibilities for meaningful activities across the curriculum that actually teach something required at your grade level. (I wince inwardly when I remember a few of the activities that I had my kids do in the name of a thematic unit, such as covering a tagboard cutout of an apple with tiny squares of red tissue paper that had been wrapped around the eraser end of a pencil and dipped in glue.)

It is also possible to choose a topic, such as "the Earth," that is too broad. (When I was participating in a professional development class in designing science-based thematic units, my first idea was "The natural and human resources of Monterey County." My instructor/coach tactfully noted that this topic was just too broad to work.) A theme needs to be appropriate to your grade level and its requisite standards, although many themes can be adapted to fit many grade levels. Ideally, the theme you choose should relate to the students' lives and at the same time challenge them to expand their horizons.

DEVELOPING ACTIVITIES FOR A THEMATIC UNIT

How did I develop activities related to agriculture in the various curricular areas? Although these activities were designed for first graders, I will include suggestions as to how they might be adapted for other grades.

Once you have decided on a theme, you can begin to think about what activities you might use to teach your unit. Remember, you can start with a few activities and build your unit and refine it over the years. My unit on agriculture began about 1990 when I thought of two math activities that I wanted to try with my first graders—reading and interpreting graphs and tables. (Because that skill is taught throughout the elementary grades and beyond, my activities could be easily adapted for higher grade levels.) In later years, I added language arts, science, and social studies lessons to my unit. It is helpful to develop a whole range of materials to draw on—you don't have to do every activity every year, and you will probably continue to refine what you do as you teach your unit several times. My agriculture unit spans the second semester for several reasons. The students' reading and writing ability is far beyond what it is in September. Our district-adopted math curriculum covers graphing during January and February. Seeds are usually planted in the spring. The timing of when you teach the units you design will depend on similar factors.

Math

Creating and interpreting graphs is one of the California math standards for first graders. Math textbooks often do not give the children adequate opportunity to work with graphs. There are few examples, and those included are usually not very relevant to my students' lives. I wanted to help my students make graphs that would have a real visual impact and would be meaningful to them.

The first graph we made was a bar graph of the agriculture-related work students' parents did. Along the bottom of the board I placed pictures of crops, as well as spaces for working "at home" and in "other jobs." Students drew pictures of their parents on 3- by 3-inch papers and then glued them above the picture that showed the area in which their parents worked. Next, the students interpreted the graph. "How many people work in lettuce?" I asked. "How many people work in strawberries? Are there more people working in artichokes or cauliflower?" The first few years I taught this unit, I had students answer the questions orally in the whole group, but sometimes only a few students responded. Later, I decided to change this activity to include reading, writing, analysis of the graph, and working with a partner. Now, after we make the graph, the students get a written questionnaire based on the chart they have made. As they work with their partners, I can observe them to make sure they understand what they are doing and assist them if necessary. This is a way to encourage all students to think and analyze; my original graphing activity did not include a way to check for understanding, and it was possible for some students to zone out during the question-and-answer period. As well as asking the questions on the written form, I can ask the pairs of students open-ended questions, such as "What can you tell from looking at this graph?" Also, I can ask them questions about their reasoning. "How did you figure out how many more people work in lettuce than in cauliflower?"

The second graphing activity I designed required me to do some research. This was about 1990; the Internet was not yet available. I envisioned a giant butcher-paper patchwork of fields with "crops" planted in them, the size of the fields and the numbers of plants proportional to their rank in acreage planted in those crops in Monterey County. I went to the Monterey County Farm Bureau to look for information. The first reports I found ranked crops by their dollar value rather than their acreage, but eventually I found what I was looking for. I calculated the size of the "fields" on a scale of ¼ square inch to the acre and then cut them from brown butcher paper. The children made lettuce, broccoli, carrots, cauliflower, celery, tomatoes, artichokes, grapes, strawberries, and flowers, one to represent each 1,000 acres planted in that crop. I took the children outside on the playground to show them approximately how big an acre is. First graders don't yet grasp the concept of 1,000, but they were all able to see that many more acres were planted in lettuce than were planted in artichokes or tomatoes. After all of the "fields" had been planted with their "crops," I cut strips of black paper to make roads to join the fields (the students decided that the roads needed cars on them, so they made the cars). Our finished graph was enormous. It took up most of the floor space in the classroom when we worked on it, and the only place big enough to display the finished graph was a wall of the school cafeteria. In subsequent years, I converted the scale to 1/8 square inch per acre—that made the size much more manageable.

Variations by Grade Level

In the upper grades, the graphs would look different, and the activities could be adapted to address different standards, as shown below using California standards as examples:

- Fourth graders are supposed to "measure the area of rectangular shapes using appropriate units" such as square meters, square kilometers, square yards, and square miles. They are also supposed to "formulate survey questions, systematically collect and represent data on a number line, and coordinate graphs, tables, and charts."
- Fifth graders are expected to "organize and display single-variable data in appropriate graphs . . . and explain which types of graphs are appropriate for different kinds of data sets."
- Sixth graders should be able to "convert from one unit to another," such as acres to hectares or square kilometers to square miles. They also should be able to "use a variety of methods such as words, numbers, symbols, graphs, tables, diagrams, and models to explain mathematical reasoning." Sixth graders could also use statistics to determine which crop is worth the most per acre or what crop has decreased in value since the previous year.

Science

According to first-grade California standards, students are supposed to know that plants need light and water to live. They also need to learn that plants use their roots to absorb water and nutrients from the soil and that plants use their leaves and sunlight to make food. They plant bean seeds in clear plastic cups and keep a journal in which they write six times over the course of 2 weeks to describe the growth of their bean plants. Observing and recording data is another first-grade science standard, and description using sensory detail is a language arts standard. Each day they write, they also draw what they observe. It is sometimes hard to convince my students that they are to draw only what they see—occasionally, I get a picture of a full-grown sunflower instead of a bean plant, or a picture of one plant with two leaves instead of three plants with two, three, or four leaves each. Occasionally, I get a journal entry that expresses feelings as well as observations ("none of my seeds has come up; I am very sad;" "my plant is really pretty, and it's going to beat Jose's plant because it's bigger"). Measurement is another first-grade standard—once the plants start to grow, students use rulers to find their height in centimeters.

Students learn about plant growth and the skills of observation and recording, but the joy I find in teaching this part of the unit comes from my students' sense of wonder at watching the miracle of a seed as it germinates and grows. I always wait to see who will notice that the seeds have started to sprout. The children come in, take their seats at their tables, and begin to read their library books as they do daily. Then, someone notices that a few of the beans have sprouted—that student excitedly comments to her neighbor, the buzz goes around the room, and there is a rush on the area by the windows. Magic has happened overnight, but it is magic grounded in reality and not in fantasy, and it is accessible to anyone with a bit of soil and a few seeds.

Variations by Grade Level

Plant growth in the upper grades can be studied in more complexity than in primary grades. Below are examples.

- For second graders, this lesson could be adapted by varying the conditions under which the seeds are planted, since one of the California second-grade standards states that students need to know that "the germination, growth, and development of plants can be affected by light, gravity, touch, or environmental stress."
- Fourth graders could make compost from plant waste. Standards for that grade level state that "plants are the primary source of matter and energy entering most food chains" and that "decomposers, including many fungi, insects, and microorganisms, recycle matter from dead plants and animals." A colleague used to bury a pumpkin after Halloween and dig it up with her students at intervals throughout the year to see how far decomposition had progressed.

- Fifth graders could use colored water to see "how sugar, water, and minerals are transported in a vascular plant." Fifth graders also must develop a question, plan an investigation, and write instructions that others can follow to carry out an experiment. They could do this in small groups, with their question based on planting and germinating seeds.

Social Studies

There are several first-grade California social studies standards that relate to the agriculture unit. Students are expected to describe "how location, weather, and physical environments affect the way people live, including their food," an important standard for an area that has been described as "the salad bowl of the world." Students are supposed to study "national holidays and the heroism and achievements of the people associated with them." (Cesar Chavez's birthday is a state rather than a national holiday, but the other criteria apply.)

For the social studies portion of my unit on agriculture, I focus on two areas: the Dust Bowl migration to California and the history of the farm-worker movement. Students find many similarities between the stories of the agricultural laborers from Oklahoma and Arkansas who came to California seeking work (many of whom settled in Salinas) and the Mexican immigrants' struggles 30 years later, some of which continue to this day.

Even though, chronologically, the story of Cesar Chavez and the founding of the United Farm Workers occurred after the Dust Bowl migration, I teach it first because it is more immediate to my students' experience. They all know people who work in the fields, whether or not their own parents do. They can relate to the injustice of having to work long hours at low pay while living under very difficult conditions, of being ridiculed for speaking their own language at school, and of not having access to restrooms and clean drinking water. I use a picture book, *Harvesting Hope* (Krull, 2003), that does a good job of portraying Cesar Chavez's early years, the struggle in the fields, and the long march from Delano to Sacramento that made the farmworkers' plight known and visible to the rest of California. Many of my students are familiar with the UFW's red flag with its black eagle and comment, "I saw flags like that when I went to a march" or "I have a flag like that at my house." We talk about what it takes to bring about changes and about Cesar Chavez's commitment to nonviolence. (Last year, as I was reading my students one of the *Chronicles of Narnia* books in which children discuss their brother's role in an upcoming battle, one boy commented out of the blue, "Cesar Chavez wouldn't have done that!") We also sing songs associated with the farmworker movement—*"De Colores,"* and in

English and Spanish, "We Shall Not Be Moved" (first graders sing "*NO!* *NO! No nos moverán!*," the latter song with great enthusiasm; I think that it appeals to the sense that one can defy authority and that there is power in numbers).

After my students have learned about Cesar Chavez, I share with them the book *Children of the Dust Bowl: The True Story of the School at Weedpatch Camp* (Stanley, 1992). Our school library has a class set of this book, enabling every student to have a copy to look at. The book tells the story of the Dust Bowl refugees and the hardships they faced as they left their lives in the Midwest behind and arrived in California, where they were met with prejudice and, in many cases, hatred. The children of these migrant agricultural workers were often turned away from California schools or told that they were too dirty or stupid to attend school. At Weedpatch, however, the "Okie" children came under the influence of a remarkable school principal, who, with the children's help, built the school from the ground up and then hired the best and most dedicated teachers in the state to work at the school. My students are fascinated by the book's many black-and-white photos of the Weedpatch camp, the children, and the school. It takes us several days to go through the book—I don't read it to them; I do a "book talk" in Spanish to explain the Great Depression, the Dust Bowl migration, and the experience of the particular children who attended the Weedpatch School. My first graders draw parallels between the Okies' experience and the Mexican American experience a generation later.

Variations by Grade Level

It would be fairly easy to adapt a study of local agriculture and of migrant workers to standards at other grade levels.

- These activities could be adapted for kindergarteners since, in California, they are supposed to learn about "the people and events honored in commemorative holidays" and "the different ways people lived in earlier days."
- Second graders are supposed to "compare and contrast their daily lives with those of their parents and grandparents," "compare and contrast basic land use in urban, suburban, and rural environments in California," and learn about "food production and consumption long ago and today."
- Third graders are supposed to know "how local producers have used natural resources, human resources, and capital resources to produce goods and services in the past and present," which would include agriculture.

- Fourth graders could make use of maps to see "how communities in California vary in land use, vegetation, wildlife." They also could compare the agricultural practices of various Native peoples in California with present-day agricultural methods.
- Sixth graders could compare present-day California agriculture and irrigation methods with those of "the early civilizations of Mesopotamia, Egypt, and Kush, in terms of . . . the location and description of the river systems, and . . . the development of agricultural techniques that permitted the production of economic surplus and the emergence of cities," since the study of ancient civilizations is part of the sixth-grade curriculum.

Language Arts

Language arts are integrated into all curricular areas of this thematic unit. Students listen to and read stories and nonfiction related to agriculture. They do different kinds of writing—answers to questions about graphs, scientific observations, responses to and summaries of literature, and thank-you notes to guest speakers. I read Lois Ehlert's *Eating the Alphabet* (1989) to my students, and they then make an illustrated alphabet book for the class with the Spanish names of fruits and vegetables. The students learn English songs that reinforce the concepts they have been learning about in Spanish.

Variations by Grade Level

Older students can read grade-level-appropriate fiction and nonfiction books as part of this unit. There are many books available that deal with farming in bygone days—Laura Ingalls Wilder's books about her childhood on the Great Plains and Lois Lenski's books about tenant farmers and migrants are some examples. You can look at your grade-level standards to see the kinds of writing that are required at each grade level. Older students can write to local agencies such as the County Agricultural Extension Service, the County Farm Bureau, or the U.S. Department of Agriculture to ask for information or invite guest speakers to visit the class.

GUEST SPEAKERS

I like to have guest speakers visit my classroom. They provide kids with a fresh perspective and a chance to enrich their knowledge of the world, as well as an occasional glimpse of careers thus far unknown to them. As part of this unit, I've had as guests an agricultural extension agent who is a proponent of organic farming and an expert in weed control, an employee of the local Center for Rural Development who teaches farmworkers how to become farmers, and a Japanese American teacher who grew up on a 40-acre farm in California's Central Valley (she brings me wonderful peaches, nectarines, and persimmons every year from the farm). I've also had as a guest a mother who works in a salad-packing plant—she provided a comprehensive description of how packaged salads go from field to grocery store, and she brought samples of packaged baby carrots, snap peas, and lettuce for the kids to try. Another mother told about working on a lettuce harvesting crew—she told my students that they needed to study hard so that they would not end up doing the kind of backbreaking labor that she did, but she also spoke of the satisfaction of seeing a whole truckload of lettuce on its way to market and knowing that she had played a part in filling that loaded truck. My students always write and illustrate thank-you notes to those who come to speak to the class.

LEARNING AS A TEACHER

Once you've decided on a theme for your unit, be on the lookout for any information that can add to your knowledge or your students' knowledge of your topic. Start a folder for newspaper or magazine articles or photos you may come across, and start a collection of links to Web sites pertaining to your topic. Seek out books that are available at your school or local public library that would be good resources for your students, and keep a list of these books so that you can check them out when you need them the next year. You may find some books that are so indispensable that you want them for your classroom.

One of the fringe benefits of preparing to teach a thematic unit is that you learn a great deal that you didn't know before about your subject, particularly if you teach the same unit over a period of years. It's been interesting to see the changes in local agriculture that I have observed in the 18 years I have been making graphs with my students. Tomatoes and carrots no longer make the "top 10." Lettuce is as plentiful as ever, but is now divided into head lettuce and leaf lettuce—the popularity of bagged salad mixes, among other factors, has caused much more leaf lettuce to be planted. The acreage devoted to wine grapes has expanded considerably. Also, 18 years ago at least half of the parents of my students worked in the lettuce fields. Now there is much more diversity in my students' parents' occupations. I have much less turnover in my class roster than I used to, possibly related to more year-round work for the parents and less need to follow the crops to other places.

WHAT KEEPS ME TEACHING

If you are going to stay in teaching for the long haul, it is important to think about what will help you to do that. My fifth and sixth years of teaching were so difficult that I think I would have left the profession had it not been for the 4 good years that preceded that period. My seventh year, I was at a new school in a new community and remembered why I had liked being a teacher. In my experience, there are several factors that can influence whether or not one stays in teaching.

Having a principal who is supportive of teachers makes a huge difference. If what I have written here describes the kind of teaching you want to do, it will be very difficult to work under someone who feels the need to synchronize everything that goes on in every classroom. A good principal can inspire teachers, foster a positive school environment, and do a lot to facilitate good teaching. For instance, my principal wants teachers to be able to observe and learn from one another, so she will take over a classroom for an hour or so if we ask her to. She listens to us. This is not to say that we can do whatever we want to, but our opinions are valued.

Finding like-minded colleagues helps a lot also. My first year of teaching, I was fortunate enough to work next door to another teacher who had taught my students the previous year. Sylvia gave me lots of good advice about classroom organization, lesson design, and wall decor. I still use her system for "stations," as she called her learning centers. Yet, as much as I appreciated all this help, I appreciated just as much the laughter we shared and her assurance that "This is a difficult class. Don't worry that you're doing something wrong." I've been at my present school for 20 years, and it is my fellow first-grade teachers who have kept me there year after year. We share teaching ideas, take turns teaching music to provide planning time for each other, and go out to lunch on Fridays. Relationships with colleagues can be a really important part of teaching, since otherwise, being in a classroom can be isolating.

Finally, it is the students and their parents who provide me with reasons to remain in teaching. I teach in an area where parents have little schooling and little money, but most of them have a great desire for their children to get an education. If you make parents welcome, if you are accessible to them, you will benefit. You may get direct help—for the last 4 years, parents have taken care of putting together my homework packets every week—but even if you don't, you will develop a sense of trust with parents that will assist you when you need their help with their children. It is the students themselves, though, who allow me to see life each year through the eyes of 6-year-olds as well as through my own, and so far this joy has outweighed everything else.

CHAPTER 6

Navigating Through Pressures to Reach High Academic Standards and Achievement

Juanita Perea

Juanita Perea was born and raised in Guanajuato, Mexico. She was 14 years old when she came to California in 1989. She worked doing different menial jobs in the Monterey Bay area, which included housekeeping, agriculture, and babysitting. When she was 17 years old, she started high school and began to learn English. The experience of being a math tutor and later an English language development tutor shaped her future professional life. After high school, she attended California State University–Monterey Bay, where she received her bachelor's degree, teaching credential, master's degree, and then a doctorate in a joint program with California State University–Monterey Bay, the University of California–Santa Cruz, and San Jose State University. She is the oldest of 16 children, although only eight are still alive, and she has a son in high school. Currently, she is the assistant director of education at Oasis Charter Public School, the only charter school in the Salinas Valley. She wants to thank some of her previous teachers—especially LeAnne Haas, Christine Sleeter, and Bob Hughes—for helping her to believe in her potential to become a teacher and a school administrator.

I had just completed the requirements for a bilingual multiple-subject (elementary) teaching credential at California State University–Monterey Bay. I was so excited! My professional mission was to be a tool to facilitate learning and to guide the students to explore different learning experiences. Ackoff and Greenberg (2008) point out that a teacher should "serve as a guide and a resource but not as one who force-fed content into students' minds" (p. 2). Serving as a guide and a resource is exactly what I was ready to do when I first entered a classroom, and I was made to believe that I was there to teach and the students to learn.

MY SCHOOL AND MY STUDENTS

On January 10, 2000, I was hired to work as a bilingual teacher for a kindergarten through 12th grade unified school district that had four elementary schools, two middle schools, and one high school. In 2000, only one elementary school in the district was under the state system called Program Improvement, which meant that the students were underperforming in the state annual standardized assessment. However, by 2006, all of the four elementary schools were classified as underperforming and were placed on the state radar as Program Improvement schools.

I accepted the job to teach for a rural school that served kindergarten through fifth grade. The school had about 500 students; most of them were bussed in from the surrounding communities. It had permanent classrooms and many portable rooms as well. The majority of students, more than 70%, were Latinos. However, the teacher population was the opposite of the student population, with the majority being White. The school had met the yearly growth targets set by the state in assessment performance until the end of the school year in 2006.

I was placed to teach in a second-grade bilingual classroom with all Latino/a students, the large majority of whom were of Mexican descent. All of the students were English language learners, and a vast majority of their parents were first-generation immigrants and had little or no knowledge of the English language. Most of the families worked in the packing companies or in the agricultural fields of the county.

During my first few years in the classroom, the curriculum provided by the district gave me the freedom within which I could develop curriculum to create a learning environment where everyone was engaged in critical thinking and problem-solving activities. However, a couple of years later, the newly adopted curriculum, as well as state and district mandates, seemed designed to kill the joy of teaching and learning, and what I always believed to be the purpose of teaching, which was to support and challenge learning.

The district purchased two language arts state-adopted curricula published by the largest companies. Bilingual education teachers were given the option to choose. We opted for the less restrictive curriculum of the two, even though it, too, was a scripted and very much prescribed curriculum. Page by page, we were told what to do and when to do it. For instance, the language program required 90 minutes of direct instruction and 30 minutes of universal access or small-group instruction. The math program required 40 minutes of direct instruction and 20 minutes of informal or formal assessment. It was up to me to be creative and innovative with how I organized the curriculum and the strategies to be used, within the prescribed structure.

The biggest challenge was to hold up high academic expectations in a learner-centered classroom, while battling against institutionalized and legitimized pressures. Those pressures included following the pacing guide, using the teacher's manuals, meeting grade-level expectations, administering standardized testing, and attending traditional professional development workshops. District administrators institutionalized and legitimized the implementation of the standardized curriculum and standardized professional training to try to ensure that all teachers and students learned the same things at the same time. Fortunately, my school administrator did not force us to follow everything that the district wanted us to do. The pressures came from the state and the district office to meet the yearly target growth as measured by the standardized assessments. Consequently, we felt pressured to focus mostly on reading, writing, math, and English language development, which were the only subjects being tested.

Since I expected every student to be prepared in every possible way to enter college in the future, regardless of all the pressures and challenges that must be overcome, I had to be creative and innovative to find a system to safely navigate through those pressures.

STARTING BY CREATING OWNERSHIP AND RESPONSIBILITY

The first and most vital goal in the classroom was to create a sense of ownership and responsibility. I believed that children could run the classroom in an orderly fashion and solve problems in a civil, competent way. Under my guidance, the students came up with classroom rules, and we had weekly class meetings to express our thoughts and feelings, to problem solve, and to find support systems that could help one another make responsible choices. At all times and in all situations, my expectations were high, yet appropriate for the group.

This worked until one day, when the students had a substitute teacher who demanded more control than I did over what they had to learn and over their behavior. Although the students were able to run their day without an adult, the substitute's expectations were very different from what we had already established. Throughout the day, the students kept a detailed list of the incidents and situations that arose in class. The next day, when I returned to class, they requested a class meeting to talk about their day with the substitute.

I guided them to express their experiences in full sentences and in a coherent sequence of events. For instance, some of them expressed concerns about being yelled at when they were not following instructions or when they were distracted during class time. Yelling is certainly not a successful way to handle classroom management, and yet the students in the class had control over their actions through self-control and self-monitoring. We later developed a list of possible ways to solve the problems; some had group solutions and others had individual solutions.

Within the list of possible solutions to their concerns, the students suggested that the substitute be fired, that she quit being a teacher, or that she be fined, which were probably impossible solutions to the issue at hand. However, my mission was for their opinions and suggestions to be acknowledged, honored, and respected. At the same time, it was my responsibility to guide them to find possible and realistic solutions to their traumatic experience with the controlling substitute. We finally came up with a solution, which was for half of the class to write letters to the substitute to let her know how they felt with the way she had treated them. The other half wrote letters to the school administrator describing the events and how people felt. In those letters, the students described how their class was run on a daily basis and acknowledged their responsibilities and duties in the classroom. By doing this, the students took ownership, responsibility, and leadership in civic participation to make their learning experience one of respect and acceptance.

We began the school year with self-selected learning experiences, which others call research projects. But people start conventional projects, and once those are finished, they are set aside, and many times, they are forgotten. Learning experiences, on the other hand, have meaning to the students; those are remembered for many years to come, and are later applied to other situations. Each student selected a research topic, and students used their observation skills, interview skills, knowledge, and resources to complete it. Each student had different academic skills, such as reading, writing, math, art, and social and cultural knowledge; my responsibility was to extend those skills and to extend their zone of proximal development. Using informal and formal assessments, I had to find out their reading level, such as fluency and comprehension; their writing abilities; and their English and their math knowledge. To find out about their cultural and social knowledge I did informal home visits; frequently, families with whom I established an open and honest line of communication volunteered in the classroom.

As the students tapped into their background knowledge to start their projects, my role was to support them to find new, critical, and in-depth information to broaden their area of interest. For instance, one of their learning experiences was to do biographies about migration issues. Another one was to write about the jobs of their closest family members. The students had to do a poster, a PowerPoint, or a question-and-answer presentation in front of their classmates. They had to use resources found in the classroom, in their home, and in their community. Some of those resources were family members who were interviewed.

At the same time, I did not ignore or neglect California state standards. As the facilitator, it was my responsibility to ensure that the key standards were addressed for all of the content areas: math, language arts, science, social studies, English language development, physical education, technology, and the arts. I combined subjects such as social studies and language arts, math and music, or an academic subject with physical education activities, in order to provide maximum exposure to interesting and challenging topics. Many of the skills that needed to be learned for one subject overlapped with another subject.

I supported and challenged the students to reach beyond the state and district academic standards. I had to keep reminding myself that the California academic standards were only a tool and not the teaching method or strategy. Those standards describe what students need to learn, but they do not dictate which pedagogical strategies should be used. For instance, the California state second-grade standards expect students to write one paragraph with at least three complete sentences. I supported those students who were ready to write two or even three paragraphs with at least five complete sentences. The reading fluency standard was 50 words per minute, and in my classroom, students were always reading at a minimum of 50 words per minute; the more advanced students read at 200 words per minute.

STUDENTS AS RESEARCHERS AND WRITERS

Keeping alive the joy of learning that was disappearing from classrooms was another conscious choice I made. Utilizing the resources available to students and their experiences across the curriculum through interviews and observations were only a few of many opportunities for students to have their voices heard. For instance, one of the learning experiences integrated language arts, social studies, technology, and art. Students were to choose a community site to research that had meaning to them and that they wanted to know more about. The students chose places such as churches, parks, transportation stations, shopping centers, grocery markets, hospitals, clinics, and support centers. Once the site had been selected, we came up with guidelines and rubrics for their presentation project.

We created guidelines with a backwards design. First, we looked at the reading and writing standards and then we came up with the minimum requirements. For instance, the paragraph had to have at least three complete sentences, with subjects and predicates in place. The research report had to have at least one paragraph addressing at least two interview questions, such as: Why did you migrate to this country? What is your greatest motivation? What type of work do you do? Why do you do that kind of work? For the presentations, the students had to have at least one visual aid, present for at least 3 minutes, and be able to answer questions from their classmates about their research. If the presenter was unable to answer the questions, then he or she had to write them down and come back the next day with the answer or simply respond, "I don't have an answer for that question" or "I did not research that subject."

We also came up with interview questions and observation checklists appropriate for the topic and for the development of the student. For instance, as a class we developed questions to ask the interviewee. Families received safety guidelines to keep the students safe when they were interviewing or observing and their input was welcomed and encouraged to improve or develop clearer guidelines. I sent home a simple questionnaire with questions such as: Who would you prefer your child to interview? What place would you like for him or her to visit? Would you have time to accompany your child during the observation? The families also participated by sharing their knowledge or expertise on the subject. For example, the students interviewed family members who had a certain skill such as those who were small-business owners, quality-control personnel in a packing company, or janitors. When interviewing or observing, the students took notes, which they then turned into sentences and later into paragraphs. I guided the students to convert their sentences into paragraphs; some were able to write one paragraph, while others wrote up to three and four paragraphs. We followed the writing process of brainstorming, drafting, editing, reviewing, and publishing their work. They used a word-processing program to type their work and were given multiple opportunities to complete their work on the computer.

I gave students disposable cameras to take multiple pictures of their community site and of the people they interviewed. Since I couldn't buy a camera for each one of them, given the limited resources, the students took turns taking the cameras home. Once the pictures were developed, I showed them how to scan the pictures, save them, insert them into a Word document, and download clip art to illustrate or decorate their writing. The students also used the Internet to do research and to download pictures about their topic. Some students were very independent, and others needed continuing support throughout their research.

The main goal of the different research projects was for the students to write about many experiences throughout the school year, and to create a book to take home with all of their own work. Throughout the school year and after each research experience, family members volunteered to come in to put together a class book with a hard-bound cover. The students took turns checking them out to take home to read and share with their family. There was one book per project for the whole class with all of the students' writing as well as a book per student with all of their writing projects from the school year.

In the different classroom learning experiences, the students were exposed to the second-grade language arts standards referred to earlier: writing three or more sentences, creating one or more paragraphs, and formulating questionnaires and checklists. They also needed to learn the writing process as well as to analyze critically and select the needed information to complete their research. One of the social studies themes was to explore community resources and to gain insight about the professions practiced in the community. The students needed to learn to use a scanner and a camera, to navigate the Web, to manage a word-processing program, and to insert art and pictures into a document. The art standard was followed when the students integrated puzzles, drawings, paintings, and design into their final products. Ackoff and Greenberg (2008) said, "in the educational process, students should be offered a wide variety of ways to learn, among which they could choose or with which they could experiment" (p. 2). I supported, guided, and challenged every student throughout and with learning experiences at their developmental stage regardless of their grade-level classification. Even though they were classified as "second graders," some of them were only writing sentences, while others were doing multiple paragraphs.

TAKING CIVIC PARTICIPATION SERIOUSLY

In an effort to maintain high academic expectations and still address real civic problems that had meaning to the students, I assisted them in finding appropriate solutions to their dilemmas by using writing to voice their concerns, as I described earlier in regard to the controlling substitute. Another situation arose because my school had to mix the students in English-only classes with those in bilingual environments to comply with the integration requirement. The education code prohibits that students be in separate classrooms all day during instructional time. One day during a class meeting, my students expressed fear about going to one particular teacher's classroom. Some of their concerns were that the teacher would always yell and scream at them and would punish them by having them sit outside the classroom or in a classroom corner looking at a wall. She did not allow the students to talk or sit next to a friend. She did not allow the students to use the restroom during class time. We brainstormed many different possible solutions to the problem. We later prioritized the list and analyzed it to decide which one or two possibilities would have the greatest success. We decided for the students individually to write a letter to the principal expressing their feelings as well as describing their experiences in detail. Each letter had to end with a request. All the students agreed that they wanted to stop going to the other teacher's class during their switch period, for an hour after lunch. In closing the letters, the students made themselves available to talk to the principal if needed.

After those letters were edited by me and then turned in to the administrator, all we had to do was to wait for a response. The students' active participation paid off, and the administrator allowed them to stop going to the other class for the rest of the school year. He also made a promise that he would talk to the teacher about the reasons why the students were no longer switching with her class. It provided great satisfaction to me to see all members of the class take responsible and respectful civic action to change their lives and those of others.

PROFESSIONAL SUPPORT MAKES A DIFFERENCE

"In most schools, memorization is mistaken for learning" (Ackoff & Greenberg, 2008, p. 1). I had made a conscious decision to make my classroom a learning environment and not a memorization of facts class. The end result of being the facilitator in a learner-centered environment was students' strong academic achievement in the district assessments as well as in the state's standardized testing. Almost every year, the students in my classroom scored substantially higher in the informal and formal assessments in comparison to all other students enrolled in the district bilingual program; in the district's four elementary schools there were about eight bilingual classes with an average of 20 students in each. Student teachers, novice teachers, district supervisors, and university student teacher supervisors visited the classroom every year in search of strategies to provide a rich and equitable learning environment for all students. There was never a secret or a trick to what was going on in my classroom. It was all about one's willingness and readiness to learn and at the same time to navigate through the institutionalized and legitimized pressures.

One of the difficult things that I had to struggle with was to find the right balance between meeting all the state standards; using the curriculum, teacher guides, and pacing maps; and still maintaining high expectations for academic achievement. It was an irony for the district to have adopted scripted curriculum, pacing guides, and rigorous standards as a way to improve student achievement, while in my 7 years of teaching I found those to be barriers for students to reach higher academic achievement. Navigating through those pressures and providing an equitable, challenging, and enriching learning environment for all students was the biggest struggle that I had to face. I always sought professional support from my university professors in the master's program. I knew that those professors were radical in their pedagogy practices and philosophy, and that was the kind of support that I needed to continue with my mission.

I recommend that teachers seek professional support and intellectual stimulation. We are the only persons responsible for our own learning and professional development. When doing this for our own growth, teachers become lifelong learners who will in turn nurture their students in the same way. Education leaders need to fight against institutionalized and legitimized pressures that work against our creativity, autonomy, intellectual growth, and professional learning.

CHAPTER 7

Hooking Students So They Don't Give Up

Stephen Stiller

Stephen Stiller is currently a teacher, certified cognitive coach, new teacher mentor, curriculum lead teacher, and math department chair at East High School in the city of Buffalo, New York. After his undergraduate studies in mathematics, education, and religion at SUNY–Geneseo, he taught algebra and geometry at several high schools in North Carolina and New York. He earned a graduate degree from SUNY–Buffalo in philosophy and has taken on roles as a professional development facilitator, district curriculum committee member, and certified technology integration specialist for Texas Instruments. Stephen has been teaching in the Buffalo Public School District for the past 7 years, and is presently teaching algebra and precalculus. When he's not at school, Stephen writes, plays, and records music with his brother.

Any teacher with any inkling of a heart is interested in motivating students. When I first started teaching math about a decade ago, "hooking" students into the subject matter and keeping them from giving up were quite challenging. I regularly found myself saying that I felt like I was trying to keep my hands on the heads of 20 or 30 students for the entire period, keeping them focused and on task. I didn't understand why I seemed to be "force-feeding" students the wonderful nourishment of knowledge, understanding, and the capacity to think. I didn't feel effective, but I didn't know how else to teach. It seemed that all I could do was continue to lecture, although I was only reaching the few students who could endure 40 minutes of listening. As long as a couple of students were responding to questions, I continued on in the footsteps of my own high school teachers.

Eventually, I had to face the fact that I didn't feel successful in my career. Holding the bar just high enough to keep administration satisfied made me feel like I was not taking my responsibilities seriously enough. I knew and still know that I could get away with doing "well enough," or I could continue to develop, change, and evolve my skills for the sake of the young people who depend on me to educate them.

In my first years, being the "sage on stage" was my main tool for not only disseminating information, but also for conducting most of the class period's "activities." These so-called "activities" were teacher-centered; whatever concept was explained or discovered was being explained or discovered by me. The instruction mostly included "chalk and talk," with brief moments of students doing more than just listening and taking notes. I felt that if I lectured with enough passion and energy, all the students would follow my every word, and at the end of the class they would all completely understand every step of whatever process was being taught and would be able to replicate and regurgitate it back exactly as I "taught" it. Of course, I was wrong. This was quite evident from my end-of-year test results. It was not that I did worse than other teachers, but that so few students gained anything close to mastery of the material.

Finally, I had to upgrade my methods so that I could feel like I was doing my job. Lecture has a time and a place and will probably be an element of daily routine for most teachers, but now I understand that is not the most effective method. Studies are abundant that show how having students sit in rows and listen to a teacher talk is not the most effective way to teach for learning. The general rule of thumb is that people can only listen for as many minutes as years they have been alive. This means that most students can only listen and retain information for 5–15 minutes of lecture at a time. Most teachers, in my experience, do not follow that rule. Instead, they often blame the students who, even though they are part of the problem, are not the ones directing the daily activities in the classroom. As teachers, we are the ones who are positioned to make change.

The thing that blew my mind was that my administration and the other faculty members were highly impressed with what I felt were poor results. They were happy that more students passed than they had expected. Although I was happy to take compliments, I was not satisfied with reaching out to a mere three students per class. I knew I needed to reach out to all students.

TEACHER ATTITUDES TOWARD STUDENTS

The Complainers

As teachers, coworkers can be a great help or a great obstacle. While sitting in faculty rooms and talking to teachers, I've found that many teachers have a negative view of students. These teachers feel that the students are not capable of performing to high standards. Comments beginning with "They can't," They won't," and "They aren't" flooded my ears from my peers and mentors. What made it worse was that I could really relate to what they were saying. They were correct about how many students don't respect homework, grades, rules, procedures, and whatnot. They were justified in having these feelings.

I also felt that if the students would just try harder and respect the educational process, our results and their lives would be greatly improved. This, of course, is and always has been true. Nevertheless, this is not what we control. As teachers, we have control of a lot in a student's life. Sure, it may only be 40 minutes a day, but it's 5 days a week for 9 months a year. We can complain all day about students, parents, and administration. Much of our complaining would be legitimate, but in the end, I have found that complaining is not useful or productive when it comes to teaching.

The Hopeful

I find myself very blessed for the few people whom I have worked with along the way who believed in not only me but also the students. I've taught in six schools and been in over a dozen more, and it seems to me that there is always at least one person who does not join in with the negative choir. There has always been at least one teacher who would warn me not to buy all the negativity. Someone was always there to remind me that I can play a positive role in many students' lives and that I can be a helpful and productive member of society by helping as many young people as I can. It is this viewpoint that helps me feel satisfied and fulfilled in my profession, rather than growing resentful and becoming one of the too many "burnt out" teachers who hate the students and their job. It is easy to fall into the mindset that the ball is in the students' court and that we as teachers are victims of the existing systems. It is also easy to pick up the ball and head for whatever goals you believe are important. As I always say to the students, "It's your life, your choice, and your future." If no one has told you that the students can, then let me do so now. Students can perform, but someone has to be there to hold the bar not too low, not too high, but just right to help that performer improve his or her abilities.

Over the years, I found myself taking a practical point of view; due to social, psychological, and various other factors, I've had to come to terms with the fact that some students may slip through the cracks, not being reached by my efforts. The important lesson that I have learned is that you never know which student is going to be the one you can reach.

After teaching for several years in the inner city, I have met plenty of students who have given me a first impression that seems to say, "I'm not interested in what you are offering." I have spent much time in classes that have mostly special education students enrolled who seem to send the same message. In some cases, this first impression was accurate, and the student was not successful. Most of the time, I can honestly say that I was misunderstanding their message. It wasn't that they were saying, "I won't" or "I'm not"; instead, what I found the students were really saying was, "I can't" or "I need help and I'm too proud to ask." What often seemed to be an unwilling student turned out to be a very willing student, once the student overcame the fear of failure he or she had gained over the years. I am certain that the students played a role in their own growth, but I would be foolish to think that my unwillingness to give up on even the most resistant students didn't play a role.

Sure, I admit that every student probably will not grasp every idea, but that is not as important as the previous truth; if I try with every student, including the ones I might want to give up on, then I'll have a chance of reaching maybe one or two of those hard-to-reach students. That is an important enough reason for me to get out of bed before the sun rises.

People Are Diverse

As we all know, people learn in different ways. Some people are better auditory learners. Even more people learn better visually. Most people can learn kinetically, and that is how most job training happens. This is also true with the teaching profession. Being a high school teacher, I learned most of the subject matter needed for my job when I was in high school. The more important lessons I utilize were learned from interactions with people. This is true because a teacher's life is about working with people, and people are very diverse. Of course, the deeper understanding of my subject matter that I gained in my undergraduate work is valuable, but not as valuable as being able to work closely with people.

Over a few years of teaching, it became more obvious that my most important skills concerned dealing with human beings and their various quirks. It's easy to say that a child cannot jump through a very specific hoop, but it's also easy to see that that specific child can jump through hoops that others cannot. We all know a student who behaves terribly in class, but does great on tests. We all know the opposite who does great in class, but fails the tests. I've met numerous students who do not perform well on multiple choice, but can write great essays or make fabulous posters. I could go on and on. The point is that the diversity of your students will require you to not only be able to find weaknesses and strengths in individuals, but also to exploit them.

The disabilities of students are often perceived as the bane of our existence, when truly they are the reason we have a job! I can't count how many times students have complained that they aren't trying because they don't know how to do the task. I always take that opportunity to explain that that is the exact reason why they are in this classroom.

Working with students' disabilities is a huge part of our job, but so is working with their abilities. By pointing out a student's strength, you help that student define his or her identity. My favorite example of this is the "bad," "rough," or "problem" child in your class. More often than not, this student is popular and rather talented at talking or working with people. I love to exploit that skill during group work by saying to that student, "I really need your help today keeping these kids on target" or "Would you help John and Marie start the activity?" This not only empowers the student, but often eliminates any disciplining you would have had to do with that student.

Our Choice

The main point here is that we teachers have a choice. We can choose to focus on the "cans" or the "cannots." It is up to us whether to think about the kids we can't reach or the ones we can. There are bookshelves of books declaring that expectation leads to outcome, and while we may never get 100% pass rates, we can reach more students and improve more lives by focusing on and seeking the positive. It is up to us to choose to talk about what we can do or what we cannot. It is up to us to say, "tsk, tsk" or "task, task." Our life, our choice.

ADOPTING COLLABORATIVE LEARNING

As I noted at the beginning of the chapter, one of the biggest challenges for me as a teacher was letting go of the role of lecturer. In the beginning of my career, all computations and ideas came out of my mouth. Every step of every solution was chosen and acted out by me. I strongly avoided leaving the board for group-work activities because I felt that they created discipline issues and a lack of rigor in the classroom. After years of feeling unsuccessful, I finally became open to other ideas (rather than teaching exactly how I was taught). It took a few powerful workshops and influential people to help me realize that I was only holding onto lecturing because that is how I learned and felt comfortable. My life was changed when someone told me never to say something a student could say. It was a complete transformation for me. Yet it took raw data and hours of reflecting to make me realize that cooperative learning reaches out to all, while lecturing reaches out only to students who are self-motivated, well-behaved, disciplined, auditory learners. I felt that I had to reach out to all students, not just those who can learn from lecture.

Once I finally got up the guts to allow the students to take control of their own education, I never went back. I certainly still lecture for at least 5 minutes a class, but my day is smoother, easier, and more fun because I am not tied to the front board. I am free to interact with my students while they interact with our curriculum. I allow students to make mistakes and learn from them. It wasn't easy to let them fall, but it was completely worth it when I watched them get up again and run.

There is plenty of research available that shows that students learn, grow, and perform better collaboratively. Being able to work with people is a major component of what employers are looking for today. Give yourself a chance to see if you like teaching through collaborative learning. It may at least prove useful as a nice break from the daily routine of "chalk and talk." Collaborative activities can make the teacher's job easier in several ways. They take stress off the throat. Like having a "warm-up" routine, collaborative lessons can free up some time for the teacher to deal with things such as discipline, phone calls, or one of the other million things that might pop up. As time passes, use of group activities also becomes much less intense for the teacher because the students are the ones doing all the talking, showing, teaching, and learning. The teacher is free to take care of individual needs and facilitate group efforts. Most important, it helps hook students and keep them hooked by putting them in control. It can even make teachers look good by improving our test results. Do an Internet search for collaborative learning benefits and you'll find hundreds more reasons to try collaborative learning.

GETTING READY

Manage Time

Although being a teacher can be one of the most rewarding and exciting jobs in the world, we all know it can also be very stressful. Stress, we also know, is not good for you or the people around you. I find it important to mention that taking time for myself could possibly be my most profound and necessary "trick of the trade."

During my first week of teaching, I went to bed super-early every night to make sure I was extra prepared for my job. I spent much of my free time doing schoolwork and preparing for the next day. I learned the hard way that our body, mind, and soul play a role in our job and that these elements need to be respected and cared for. My first week was depressing and stressful because I felt that my life had been lost. I am thankful that I quickly learned that making time to have fun and relax not only recharged me during the school day, but also made me happier overall. I find being consumed with my work can feel wonderful because I am doing a service for others, but if I do not make a point to take care of myself every day, it shows in my ability to perform.

With that being said, it also is important to mention that planning is correlated with performance. The more I plan for a lesson, the more confident I feel. I look forward to lessons more when I feel they are pieces of work that I can take pride in. When I rush and plan in 5 minutes, I find that it shows not only in the quality of the structure of the lesson but also in my implementation. The more thorough the lesson plan, the more capable I am at dealing with the details of the class period. The better I deal with the details, the more opportunities I have to hook students and keep them from giving up.

When I rush planning, I usually only include the facts I will be including in the day's lesson. At a bare minimum, I always make sure to have visuals ready for the next day because I understand that most people learn better visually than they do auditorily. When I take my time, I tend to include well-thought-out activities that allow for my lessons to be more "student-centered," "hands-on," and "kinetic." This causes the students to be more likely to get interested in the subject matter, and thus "hooked." If I really take my time, I often am able to come up with an ultra-powerful discovery lesson. The point is that lessons tend to hook many more students when I put my heart into them.

Develop Activities

There are plenty of activities already designed that can be very useful to help a teacher become more of a facilitator than a lecturer. There are at least two places to obtain ideas for activities, besides a textbook. The Internet is full of ideas that you can at least use some part of in your efforts to get away from the board or the overhead projector or PowerPoint. Your coworkers have a plethora of potentially useful ideas and activities. The method of "beg, borrow, and steal" is my most powerful tool as an educator. Most teachers I know love to help, and most teachers have several ideas that can help you do your job more easily and effectively. My favorite ways to develop ideas are through the creative process; by using my imagination or brainstorming with others, I have found myself enjoying my craft.

Over the years, I have found a few activities especially useful, but it depends on what you have available. I have always loved using "white boards" in class. If your school doesn't already have small dry-erase boards for individual student use stashed away somewhere, they are easy enough to make with a little help from your local hardware store. Maybe your school has wet-erase manipulatives, projectors, or interactive digital boards, or other useful items. I am often surprised by what is hidden away in cabinets and on shelves in the building. Find whatever materials you can and work from there.

With large paper, I love having the students make posters to put in the room and hallways. Posters give me the opportunity to check for understanding, get students active, and help individuals better deal with peers. Posters are especially powerful because students feel ownership of a topic if they have work displayed that demonstrates their ability to work with that topic. The posters can then be used as a tool to review for tests, reminding students of strategies, formulas, and vocabulary. Also, not that the true goal is to impress administrators, but displaying exemplary student work makes it obvious that you are teaching constructively in your classroom.

One of my favorite activities is having students make posters of the four representations of a relationship (situation, table, graph, and rule). Posters can cover a large range of topics, from algebra to calculus. Moreover, students can make mathematical representations of their own situations, rather than some word problem from a book. Allowing students to use their imagination and creativity gives them an opportunity to really understand the topic because they are the ones generating the specifics. By looking at one another's posters, students are evaluating for accuracy, making comparisons, and learning from their peers. This practice often prompts students to take more pride in their work than they might have if all of the work was on a worksheet. Some students even admit that they enjoy working with peers to make posters.

Even if your school has no resources to offer, there are still plenty of different kinds of note-taking and journaling methods that can be used regularly to add a little flavor to an otherwise bland unit plan. Getting the students to talk about your topic of the day does not require any materials, but is one of the most underestimated and powerful things a student can do in the classroom. Setting up activities that prod the students to talk to one another about the subject matter gets them thinking and sharing. Getting the students to be the ones doing the thinking and talking often gets them "hooked" on the topic because they are no longer just passive listeners; they are active participants in the educational process. They are the ones generating the situations, dealing with the details, asking the questions, answering the questions, and evaluating for accuracy. This is very different from a class-long lecture. Making the students the prime actors makes sense, since they are the ones taking the test.

Plan the Steps for a Lesson

Once you know what is available to you and what kind of activity you are going to do, it is time to break the lesson down into accomplishable tasks that make meaningful connections. Whatever your lesson might be, there will be steps that must be taken by the students to accomplish the task. My district endorses a process of "I do, we do, you do" in daily activities. Whatever your steps might be, planning these out in advance is more useful than one might think. By this, I do not only mean breaking the lesson down into objectives and closure and the like, but actually breaking each activity down into smaller objectives that you know will be accomplishable tasks. Even if I know the steps in my head, writing them down helps me organize and go deeper. I can then break the steps down into even smaller steps. This makes it easy to preplan prompts to help students along in the process. These prompts are easy to have ready by simply changing the facts or directives you would say into questions you could ask. For example, when you divide a number, say 12, by a fraction or a decimal, say ½, why is your answer always larger than the number being divided? The more time I put into this analysis and synthesis process, the more students I can reach, get hooked, and keep hooked.

Implementing Collaborative Learning

Prepare for Activities

Taking time to set up for the lesson has been underestimated by many teachers, myself included. I understand that we often do not have time for one reason or another, but taking time to prepare not only the lesson, but the environment is helpful in several important ways. I feel better about the upcoming lesson when I have the visuals set up, the desks how I want them, the manipulatives on the desks, and whatever else I need to feel ready and prepared for class. I think students can tell if I feel like I'm peddling a worthless product or offering a valuable tool by my actions and from how much effort I put in the lesson. During my first years of teaching, I think I underestimated both how much students can tell when I take pride in my teaching and also how influential a role model I often am.

Once the room is prepared and class starts, I find that it makes life so much easier to have a routine. My routine involves checking their homework while they are doing whatever "warm-up" or "ticket-in" has been assigned. A review problem or an anticipatory problem is visible and in the same place every day when they walk in the room, so they know what to do by the second week of school. This gives me time to deal with any issues that may be going on with the students, school, or myself.

Bounce-Peers-Prompts

Group work can be exhausting, especially at first, but from my experience, the students get better at working in groups with practice. During the first several group activities with a class of freshmen, I have found that they tend to sway off topic in their conversations. I make it a point to look like I am evaluating their performance, listening in with my grade book in hand. To motivate students in the beginning, I often have to chant, "He's here, he's working. She's here, she's working. He's doing nothing, he's getting nothing." After a few rounds of this, most students pick up on the fact that they are accountable for their actions. Moreover, since you aren't sustaining a lecture, you are free to help motivate and assist the students who need extra attention.

After facilitating a few hundred or so activities, a pattern emerged in my lessons that I call "bounce-peers-prompts." "Bouncing" means to swiftly move about the room from group to group or individual to individual. Bouncing around the room is easier when you are working with 5 or 6 groups of students rather than with 30 individuals, but it is possible with individuals. I have learned the hard way that it is easy to stay with one group or person during this process. The key to making this process work is visiting each group several times throughout the class period. The "peers" and "prompts" part of the process make it possible to move away from a group quickly and get more opportunities to revisit groups.

On the first round of bouncing, I make sure the students have done or are doing the first step of my plan, which is visible. For example, I'll ask all the students to make a graph. If they are not trying, I motivate them by asking if they can draw the coordinate plane. If they are trying and are stuck, then I break down the task into smaller parts by asking if they can draw an x-axis. I prompt them to help them start the smaller step and make sure to check on them the next time I am around. If I have to, I can break it down further and ask them to draw a horizontal line. If they can't do anything, then I ask a partner to help. Once most of the students are done with the first step, I bounce around to make sure the students are accomplishing the second step, and so on. When students fall behind, I either help them or point them to their peers.

The "peers" part of the process involves encouraging students to work with one another as you bounce around the room. If a student is stuck on a step, then before I try to help, I like to try to find a group member who can help. If none of the other members of the group knows what to do, then I get them talking by asking questions, and I move on. Tactics such as asking a random member of the group what the group's question is pushes group members to stay on the same page and work with one another.

Encouraging group members to help each other is efficient when you are trying to get to the other groups in the room. Students are often enthusiastic about helping others with something they know. Not only does it make students feel good about themselves when they can show someone something, but it also keeps them hooked into the subject matter. I love when they get angry while defending their viewpoint because it gives me an opportunity to help them learn to control their emotions during discourse. Furthermore, they develop an attitude and identity of being capable, which keeps them from giving up. I can remember dozens of students who tended to be disciplinary challenges because of their surplus of energy. In most cases, asking them to help others or take on a responsible role turns them into a super-tutor. I often get to help them develop their skills at being professional and polite in their interactions.

When I find a student who is stuck and there are no quick fixes like pointing to posters or a nearby peer who can help, it is time to "prompt" the student or group. For example, I know there are certain areas that a student who is being introduced to equation-solving might get stuck on. I know that they often will not know how to eliminate a constant. To solve "$x+5=7$", I'd ask a series of questions: "Is x by itself? What is happening to it? What is the opposite of adding five? If I do something to this side of the equation, what should happen to the other side?" It is convenient to have several prompts ready to go for the "sticky parts" of the activities that we might anticipate students getting stuck on, but it is also necessary to be able to think of the necessary prompt for unexpected situations. The tactic I have found useful is simply turning whatever statement you want to tell them into an open-ended question you can ask them. Instead of stating, "Write your name on the paper," I ask, "How could you let me know that this paper is yours?"

Regathering Attention

The most important component to make collaborative learning successful is having a method to get the whole class's attention at the beginning of the class or after they have started working. This is needed when several students are stuck at the same step of the process, when the class is getting too loud, for closure, to redirect, or when any other whole-group issue comes up. A method that has worked for me in gaining the class's attention involves a three-step process. In the first step, I say something like, "May I have your attention please? I now have the attention of 10 percent of the room." I don't yell, but I project my voice. Then, I say something like, "May

I have your attention, please? I now have half of the class's attention." After a breath, if there are still students talking, I finally say something like, "This is my third attempt. May I have your attention, please? I now have the attention of everybody except . . ." At that point, as I obviously am looking around the room, most people get quiet. If one or more individuals are still talking, then it is time to move the loudest one into the disciplinary process. It is rare, in my experience, to get to that point.

This exact process is not necessary, but what is necessary is a set of steps that will always lead to having the group's attention. Especially if done with a smile, I know this three-step process can get the attention of a rowdy bunch of freshmen, seniors, or teachers. I always tell other teachers that they need to find a way that works for them and they feel comfortable with, but I found out the hard way that you must have some routine in place.

The Method's Effectiveness

If done correctly, a teacher can "bounce" around the room several times in half an hour, making plenty of stops along the way to help each group or individual get through the steps that have been clearly and visually laid out. Promptly redirecting, reassigning, questioning, motivating, disciplining, and moving on allows for the teacher to deal with issues as they arise while students continue to learn. The process of "bounce-peers-prompts" helps me avoid feeling like I am trying to keep 30 students in their seats with their eyes on me listening. Instead of working with chalk, I am bouncing around the room working with humans. I'm getting the students on track with the daily objectives, helping them learn to work with each other, questioning groups, and bouncing to the next group. I am prompting the students to actively learn, not just to listen. By letting the students do the talking, teaching, and tutoring, I have put the educational responsibility in their hands. I am free to facilitate, motivate, and discipline.

WHAT DO WE DO WHEN STUDENTS WON'T?

Motivation

As I mentioned earlier, it is inevitable when you are working with hundreds of students that many of them will not easily comply with your wishes. It is natural for people to be lazy, procrastinate, and not stay on task. When these issues arise, as we know they will, I have found that it is very important not to take it personally. Dealing with lethargic students is part of our job, but many people get upset at the students for faults that exist in themselves. If we can accept human weaknesses as part of our routine, we will be less likely to take it personally and get upset. This will lead to much smoother interactions and much more productive efforts at motivation.

To motivate students with candy or stickers might be fun, but I do not wish to teach them that the goal of the educational process is those rewards. The goal of education is to help develop students. I have no intentions of implying that they are doing the work for me, their parents, or the school. They are doing the work for themselves. I take every unmotivated student as an opportunity to help. If learning is not reason enough, then getting a diploma often is. I let the students know that I make the same amount of money no matter how well they do or don't do. I make it crystal clear that the reason they are trying to understand this topic is for them, not me. If not for their own mental development, then to get a diploma that will enable them to make more money than those who do not. If I find that the whole class is not motivated, then I take the opportunity to have a quick discussion about why we are in school. I like to take them along a logical path of thought; doing the work will help them pass or do well, which will lead to a job or college acceptance, which will lead to their earning enough money for a house, car, to support a child, or whatever might be desired. I let them know that I tried in school so that I wouldn't have to try so hard after school to survive. I make sure they understand that getting involved will lead to opportunities, while defiance will not hurt anyone but themselves. I try to be positive by saying things like "keep doors open," rather than "you'll never get a job." I repeatedly let them know that success is truly reachable, but only if you reach. My favorite thing to say, as I mentioned earlier, is that it's "your life, your future, your choice."

Discipline

Often, disciplining is the most rewarding part of my job. Due to an individual's emotions, home life, or one of many other factors, all students have bad days and some students have mostly bad days. I have found it to be extremely important not to take this personally, either. I have gotten myself and many students upset by taking their issues personally and becoming noticeably upset. Now I rarely go home upset or annoyed because I realize that all I can do is my best with what I have right now. This disciplinary attitude has helped me get a multitude of students back on track who probably would have been kicked out of the room if I let my emotions direct my actions. By keeping a caring smile on my face during disciplinary procedures, I have re-hooked many students back into the lesson who probably would have given up otherwise.

It is of great importance to have a set of steps that will lead to compliance. If you can be positive during these steps, I have found that students often come out of the process more motivated than when it started. The key is that once the student has pushed past all of your initial steps, when it comes time to have an individual conversation (which you can do if the students are working in groups and not waiting for your next paragraph), I strongly endorse the "sandwich method." Step one is the top bun: a positive hello, a rapport-building statement that calms the student and lets him or her know you are not mad or upset, but rather, on the same team. The meat of the sandwich is the plan so the student can still accomplish something. The bottom bun is a motivating sentence like, "You can do it." I might say something like, "You are obviously a leader. People obviously like you. That's why it's so easy for you to get people who need to pass this class distracted. When you work, others follow your lead. I'll throw this write-up away if you use your powers for good." Giving them the initial energy boost helps the process go much smoother than calling them out in front of their peers. There are many ways to make it specifically personal for that student, and when done with care, it has been a very useful tool in building rapport. Using this positive interaction burger, I have built many wonderful relationships with students who might have become stresses in my life if I had dealt with their situations negatively, which is often very natural for an over-stressed teacher. By focusing on strengths rather than weaknesses, I have helped numerous students succeed in my class who are notoriously unruly and unsuccessful in other teachers' classes. The differentiating factor is love. By helping those who are acting like they do not want help, I am following the Golden Rule. By repaying a rude comment with efforts to help, I defuse the student's emotions. I doubt we'll reach them all, but if we keep putting our hearts into our very important job, then we can hook more and more students into the subject matter and keep them from giving up, even if they think they want to.

CONCLUSION

I have met plenty of teachers who admit that they lecture at the students for 40 minutes a day, yet still blame the students for not achieving. They believe that their duty is to say each truth once, and the rest is up to the student. I know from experience that when I assign accomplishable tasks and try my best to motivate students with thoughtful questions, I usually get more "aha" moments. I feel that the students respect us for respecting them enough to trust them with their own education. Rather than declaring the facts from behind a podium, we must first believe that the students can accomplish our goals, and then we must engage the students in working toward the curriculum-based goals. We must have a plan in place that we feel good about, and we must be ready to motivate our students toward learning. Lecture has gotten the job done time and time again (and still has its place), but the more I move around the classroom and involve the students in their own education, the more students get hooked into the lesson. The more students I make an effort to hook into the lesson, the better I feel about how I am spending my days. When I am feeling remorse about the multitude of students whom I could not reach, I remember that teaching is a path and a process. I remember that I am trying to be more effective at my craft and am putting in significant effort for the sake of helping more people . . . just like you are right now.

PART IV

Connecting School and Community

Have you ever heard a teacher complain that his or her students are hard to teach because their parents don't care about education? If so, have you ever followed up and asked the teacher how she or he knows the parents don't care? Did the parents actually say that they don't care about education? Usually, teachers make assumptions about how much parents and the community support education based on the extent to which parents show support in middle-class ways, such as coming to school during open house and helping students with homework. But in high-poverty communities, immigrant communities, or other marginalized communities, there may be a huge psychological gulf between the school and the community. Here is an illustration.

Several years ago, one of us (Christine) had teacher candidates working in a community center that served mainly low-income African American families as a vehicle for helping her students get to know the community. While tutoring children after school, three White teacher candidates became intrigued as they overheard the African American mothers talk at length about how much they valued education, and wished that the teachers in the school their children attended (which was right across the street from this center) would communicate more with them. These mothers demonstrated their care by bringing their children to the community center for tutoring on a regular basis. The next semester, Christine was supervising student teachers in that very same elementary school. There, she heard teachers grumble about how the parents didn't seem to care about education. She wondered why the teachers didn't just walk across the street, where they could talk directly with the mothers who brought their children to the center for after-school tutoring.

We realize that high-poverty communities often experience debilitating problems that include violence and drugs; students may have family members who are incarcerated; unemployment may be rampant and families unstable. And yet, there are also adults in high-poverty communities who work with young people and would like to have working relationships with teachers and schools. Describing what they called "urban sanctuaries," McLaughlin, Irby, and Langman (1994) explored the diversity of organizations that exist for youth. Some are well known, such as Boys and Girls Clubs. Organizations that are sponsored by churches or park and recreation departments may also have some visibility to schools. The researchers go on to explain that "most diverse of all are the unaffiliated, grass-roots organizations—the dance troupes, tutoring centers, theater groups, sports teams, and social clubs—that arise out of communities and draw their definition and energy from the neighborhoods they serve" (p. 9). Often, teachers are unaware of their existence. But the adults who work with children and youth in such organizations are usually highly attuned to their lives and can be powerful allies as well as community educators of teachers.

By "community educators," we mean people who can help teachers better understand the communities in which they work, the students they work with, and resources that are available in the community. Ginwright (2010) defines *community* as "a consciousness of the interrelatedness one has with others. This conceptualization of community is rooted in political, cultural, and economic histories as well as contemporary struggles in which people collectively act to make meaning of their social condition" (p. 77). Outsiders to a community in which there is concentrated poverty tend to attribute the community's problems to its residents, and are often oblivious to forms of institutional racism and classism that have shaped its circumstances (see Anyon, 2005), as well as survival and advocacy strategies within the community.

Adults who work with children and youth are usually highly aware of problems such as lack of jobs available to their parents, inadequate health-care services, and how budget cuts affect local recreation opportunities, and of how these systemic problems, coupled with rampant negative images about youth of color and/or from poor communities, impact how children and youth see themselves. They are also aware of available grassroots resources, local social action campaigns, community arts initiatives, religious organizations, and other resources that enable young people to seek refuge, share their lives, "and rebuild their identities in a way that inspires justice and activism" (Ginwright, 2010, p. 80). Such community resources maintain an identity that is separate from school when children and youth experience school as negative factor in their lives. Teachers who are willing to step out of the comfort zones of school and classroom, into the community, can powerfully relearn their students, students' families, and students' communities—and in so doing enhance their effectiveness and satisfaction.

In Part IV, two teachers discuss their work with communities in which they teach in relationship to these issues. Joanne Rickard-Weinholtz teaches at the Tuscarora Indian Elementary School on the Tuscarora Nation. She explains what it means for an oppressed community to survive, and the necessity of Native American children learning their own community's history of strength and survival so that they will be able to resist the disempowering Eurocentric perspective of schooling. She then goes on to tell stories of how she expanded her classroom to include the community, and the positive impact of community curriculum on children.

Middle school teacher Gina DeShera shares her experiences of breaking down the wall between the classroom and the community, specifically with the low-income Mexican and Mexican American community in which she teaches. She is not of Mexican descent herself, and grew up in a largely White community. Therefore, as she explains, the first part of the process of building connections with historically marginalized communities of which one is not a member is to examine oneself, and recognize how one's own experience can get in the way. She then goes on to detail various levels of engagement that teachers can have meaningfully with the communities in which they teach.

CHAPTER 8

Teaching Culture to Build Confident Learners

Joanne Rickard-Weinholtz

Joanne Rickard-Weinholtz is a citizen of the Tuscarora Nation and Turtle Clan member. She is the culture teacher at the Tuscarora Indian Elementary School within the territories of the Tuscarora Nation. She attended the elementary school where she now teaches, and graduated from the Niagara Wheatfield School District, in which her school is located. Her undergraduate degree is in business administration from the Rochester Institute of Technology, and she earned a master's degree in history from The University at Buffalo, SUNY.

Knock, knock. "Come on in, Joanne. Have a seat." Even to this day, I detest being called to the principal's office because of the negative connotation embedded in my mind as a child. When I got a call that the principal wanted to see me, I knew right away what it was about. I had handed in a field trip request. Field trips were always a negotiation.

I had put in a request to take my sixth-grade class to our local lacrosse-stick manufacturing business located within the Tuscarora Nation territories. I wanted the students to know this tradition within our culture, history, and community. Most of the students play lacrosse. Lacrosse is an indigenous game, and Haudenosaunee people believe it was a gift given by the Creator. What better way to connect the students full circle in their experience of lacrosse?

The business was owned and run by a Tuscarora elder who was also a Lacrosse Hall of Fame honoree. He still made the sticks by hand from hickory in a beautiful old barn that was in his family. I knew it was impor-

Teaching with Vision, edited by Christine E. Sleeter and Catherine Cornbleth. Copyright © 2011 by Teachers College, Columbia University. All rights reserved. Prior to photocopying items for classroom use, please contact the Copyright Clearance Center, Customer Service, 222 Rosewood Dr., Danvers, MA 01923, USA, tel. (978) 750-8400, www.copyright.com.

tant to take the students on this trip to appreciate what was in our back yard and to get to know elders who were the foundation for the youth of our community.

I hurried along the dark hallway in the old section of the school. The same dark brown asbestos-laden tiles crept up from the floor to the walls. These were the same halls I had walked as a child attending the school for my elementary education. I had never been called to the principal's office. I like to think I was a stellar student. The reality was that I was probably too scared to challenge authority in any way. I wasn't allowed to express who I was as a young indigenous person.

Here I was, a fairly new teacher. You can always tell a new teacher because their shoes click-clack down the hallway. New teachers wear what is fashionable, not necessarily what is best for their feet. Today, I wear black polished shoes that create no sound, with chiropractic insoles to lend support. I took pride in getting to the office right away, because you should always show respect.

TAKING AN ALTERNATIVE APPROACH

When I entered, the principal extended his hand to the ugly, fake-leather green chair opposite his desk, while he stood with his hand on his hip, smiling. He was a thin man with graying blond hair who had kept in shape by chasing students throughout his career all over the "rez" (short for reservation, meaning our Tuscarora Nation's territories). Behind him and out the windows was a gorgeous northeastern fall day. The sun was shining brightly, with the trees swaying and delicately scattering the spectacularly colored leaves of autumn.

Snap. I had to refocus myself from the beauty beyond the windows to the reality of the principal's grin. I knew this could not be good if he had that special little grin. I knew that, for some reason, we had established this relationship in which he absolutely, positively delighted in telling me "no" just to watch my reaction. He knew what emotional buttons to press to watch for the most entertaining response.

As a young Tuscarora person, I grew up with clearly defined ways of "protecting the line"—protecting the line of what was acceptable to say and what I would not tolerate; protecting the line of your land, so no one encroached or claimed land that was not theirs; protecting your identity as an indigenous person of Turtle Island, or as others refer to it, North America. Most important in the academic setting is to create the opportunity to empower students, so that they may be the next generation to protect the lines.

He picked up the field trip request and with that oh-so-familiar half-smile said, "Sorry, Joanne, no way I can fund this trip. There is no money for the bus," as he gently let the request fall to his desk. It was like that moment in the movie where the orchestra plays a climactic combination of strings while the paper gently glides to and fro until it alights on the desk—followed by a fist smashing the desk and flipping it over. *Snap.* Nothing like that happened. He stood there grinning while I reflected on what he said. Always remember to reflect, so that it gives you time to think.

Once more I clarified his point by restating, "No money for a bus? So we cannot go on this trip in our back yard because we cannot afford a bus to take the students less than three-quarters of a mile from the school? Is this correct?" A moment of quick reflection, and I said, "That's ridiculous! I can't believe there is no money to go less than three-quarters of a mile from the school here!"

As you can see, I was young, ambitious, and had very little finesse. All principals must balance a budget and a variety of requests. I could feel my hands grasp the metal edges of the ugly dark-green chair as I became increasingly frustrated by the ludicrous nature of the situation. We have money for the most frivolous of things in life except for the children. Internally, I was telling myself to stay calm and think of another way around this. My internal dialogue was saying, "Okay, Joanne, stay calm, think, reflect, be creative, but most of all think of the kids. You can do it; you can think of another approach."

He stood there once more with his hands on his hips and a half-smile on his face, reiterating, "There is no money for a bus; whether you go a half of a mile or 15 miles, the price is the same."

Inside, I was beyond furious; I was livid and nothing was going to stop me. The students deserved to go and learn what was in their back yard. I was not concerned about the state standards because I knew there were plenty of writing, social studies, math, and art opportunities to create from this trip. I began to tick off in my head alternative strategies to get around the "lack of funding." No one was going to stop me; we were going on this field trip. Always remember in the race of life, keep your sights on the goal, and figure out another way around the hurdles put before you. You don't have to jump each hurdle; sometimes you need to take another route.

"No funding, huh?" I said. "So, funding for the bus is the only reason, otherwise we could go on this trip?" His response was, "Absolutely." This was all I needed. . . . I struck with a big smile on my face: "Well, then we will walk!"

"Walk?" was his only response.

"Yes," I said. "We will walk to the lacrosse-stick manufacturing site. In fact, with your permission, we will make the entire experience a walking learning trip along the way."

What could the principal say?

As much as he enjoyed sparring with me, he was willing to let me go and try this new adventure. His many years in administration had given him the wisdom to know that this trip was a great opportunity for the students.

With permission slips from parents in hand, we began an awesome fall walk that included not only the lacrosse manufacturing site but also a nature walk to recognize the sycamore tree in the school yard that we pass, followed by the walnut trees, the neighbor's boxer dogs, some shag bark hickory trees, a stop at the local church for a visit and tour, a viewing of a copy of a painting of a Tuscarora man done by the well-known artist George Catlin before he traveled west to paint the indigenous people of the Plains, a stop at the Snipe Clan chief's log cabin homestead, a break to munch on grapes that would be picked and sold to Welch's for grape juice, and the lacrosse-stick manufacturing site. Next, we walked to the only other log cabin on the rez, where my parents joined us to share an oral history, followed by the story of the Hall of Fame player and how his clan came to be among us. Yes, this walking trip turned out to be so much more than a visit to the lacrosse-stick manufacturing business.

Today, I am happy to say that this walking trip in the fall continues. The stops have changed here and there, along with the passing on of some of the elders. The children in my first classes are now young adults, some in college, some are already parents of the next generation, but every time they go by the log cabin, they now are the keepers of our oral histories to share with their little ones.

How easy it would have been to agree to no trip due to lack of funding for the bus. This was a fight not for a bus, but for our young people to view our community through another lens, one of seeing the beauty of the Earth through the trees and the black walnuts that stain your hands for days; a lens that helps our young people see what it means to gain in patience through a walking experience rather than being picked up and taken to the doorstep of our destination. It was a trip than helped the students understand when my dad told the story of walking all over the rez, in a different world and time from today. So never give up; just find another way to reach the path you know your students need.

There are always times of tough choices, both professionally and personally and those that are intertwined. Remember that the role of the principal is to oversee, guide, and make sure you are on track. If you are successful, the principal will come to support and believe in you when you need it.

Later in my career, the very same principal called me back to the office one day. By now, I was getting the hang of being a teacher and the trips to the office to discuss scheduling and request various items or trips. Now, we still had our ups and downs, as any principal-teacher relationship does. Still, those ugly fake-leather green chairs sat opposite his desk.

PURSUING A DREAM OF
TEACHING CULTURAL HISTORY

This time, the trip to the office was not for me to discuss scheduling or request an item or trip. The principal revealed his plans to retire and his wish that I would consider becoming the next principal.

Actually, the reality of the situation smacked me dead in the face. I had always told my friends over dinner throughout our careers how you should be part of the solution and not add to the problem. Well, here it was—the grandest opportunity to be part of the solution, to be the person who helps steer the ship of education in our community, to bring the best to the young people of our nation, to be at the helm of opportunity. This was not a decision that I would take lightly. I thanked him for believing in me and told him I would take some time to think about it.

I applied and was accepted into a local university's graduate administrative program. I began taking classes toward my administrative degree when I decided to have an honest discussion with myself: Was this the path I wanted? Would this best meet the needs of what I wanted to do in education? Was this the change I wanted? What route would best serve the students? What is in the best interest of my students?

These were tough questions for me to answer. When I finished my undergraduate degree in business, I promised myself I would never go back to college unless I went back for something I believed in and truly wanted. Was this what I wanted?

I marched myself into the principal's office and willingly sat in the fake-leather green chair before he could offer it. I said, "*Nyaweh* (thank you) for thinking and telling me I might make a great principal, but that's not my dream job." I explained that my dream job is to become a culture teacher who works with classes all day long to educate the young people of our nation in our indigenous and Tuscarora history and culture. I would be able to accomplish this while still meeting the demands of the New York state standards.

I wanted young Tuscarora students to be knowledgeable about our history and culture. I wanted the young people of our community to learn our history and that of the indigenous people of the Americas. Throughout my life, people have inquired what am I? What is my nationality? Once people know you are Native American, the questions begin. Sometimes you feel like a walking museum. Most people mean well, while others challenge you in ways you must be prepared for.

I had left my career as a banker to be a part of the solution and begin to pursue my dream. When I attended elementary school, there were no indigenous teachers, no mention of our heritage, no acknowledgment of any kind about who we are or our history. Years prior to my attendance at the school, there was a man who taught culture and history. Also, starting in the 1970s, there was an elder woman who taught the Tuscarora language for many years. Unfortunately for my age group, we missed both opportunities. I knew that once students left our elementary school, they would learn who discovered what from a Eurocentric perspective and "how the west was won." I convincingly described a position that would teach history from a multicultural perspective while addressing the New York state standards. I give accolades to the principal and Chiefs Council for taking the risk of creating and believing in the dream of empowering our young people of the nation with the knowledge of our history, the relationship to the Confederacy, along with other indigenous communities and the world at large. First, foremost, and always, the parents and family members are the young people's teachers.

Remember the old saying "Be careful what you wish for." I was now living the dream. Of course, the dream is just that—a dream; the reality is slightly different. I had no model to go from, no curriculum, no book, no classroom, no desk, no chair, nothing; plus, I had to negotiate a slice of the schedule from precious classroom time. I was basically naive, but I had unending belief that this was right and what was best for students. This new position was my dream for the young people of my community. I asked myself once more, "What is in the best interest of my students?"

Soon, the principal found a forgettable wooden desk from the 1960s; next was the chair. Now you must envision this bright orange, fake-leather chair on four wheels that has a wraparound 2-inch-thick, U-shaped back that was used by the community clinic doctor for observing patients. This was not the chair of a school educator but rather that of a doctor seeing patients from years ago! Once more, that old half-smile appeared when the principal was wheeling this ugly, fake-leather orange chair down the hall! The principal proudly told me how he climbed into the dumpster and retrieved the chair. This chair was not going to deter me from my "dream job." Always pick your battles, weigh your options, and make your choices with the end goal in mind.

Then he placed me in the corner of the hall by the dark corkboard. There I was, with my desk and the ugly, fake-leather orange chair, yet armed with the passion that these young students were going to learn our history and culture from an indigenous perspective. I took a firm stand for space within the academic day for what to me is the most important subject that can be taught in the course of the year. It is critical for students' identities to be recognized and acknowledged, whether they are on the rez or located in an urban setting. Little did I know that with the growth of the program would come the development of a room and space for indigenous art, history, and cultural artifacts.

PROTECTING THE LINES
OF LEARNING

I still find it very difficult to articulate this narrative in a way that does justice to the most trying struggles within the culture teacher position. Just like deciding to do a walking field trip, I took an alternate path and begin to develop my position. This position would empower students. Once students are rooted in who they are, the learning may begin. Again, I remind myself to ask, "What is in the best interest of my students?"

What is in the best interest of my students is determined by asking myself, "Can I give better than what I have done?" For example, we could talk about our community, but with a little bit of effort I can take the students on a field trip to a specific place within the community. Another example may be to have a guest come in or to get a video of what we are learning about, or better yet to create an interactive lesson where the students become the teacher and so on. Lessons do not have to be Hollywood productions, but they should be ones that students buy into and want to think about and be a part of intellectually. Personalizing and relating the lesson to students' lives is powerful and always "in the best interest of my students."

For Native American students, this is critical because the Americas are our homelands. We are indigenous to Turtle Island. I am here to add to the knowledge that our young people get from their families and to put our history in context. Some things you have to stay firm on, no matter what obstacles are put before you.

According to the late Chief Elias Johnson (1881) who wrote a book entitled *Legends, Traditions and Laws of the Iroquois or Six Nations and History of the Tuscarora Indians*, we as Tuscaroras originated in what became New York State and were part of the original nations of the Iroquois, or Haudenosaunee (the People of the Longhouse or Completed House). We migrated south eventually, settling in what is today North Carolina. With colonial encroachment and the Tuscarora War, our ancestors' choice was to be killed, captured, and sold into slavery, or to migrate back home.

We as the people of the nation today represent the descendants who walked back home north into the Haudenosaunee Confederacy. Our children represent cultural survival and must be empowered through knowledge.

Tuscarora was the sixth nation to join the Confederacy in the early 1700s. An oral tradition I have been told comes from my father, Eli Rickard, Bear Clan. He was told the story by his father, the late Clinton Rickard, founder of the Indian Defense League of America (IDLA), who was told by a woman from Onondaga by the name of Snow.

The story goes that there was a group of Tuscarora trying to escape from the European colonists in the middle of the night. They had taken tree limbs and were silently floating past a fort when one of the babies began to cry. The mother could not stop the baby from crying, so she was forced to drown the baby for the group's survival.

As educators, it is vital to be clear about what you are fighting for, because there is always a cost. You need to ask yourself if you are willing to pay the price. The oral history of the Tuscarora is a powerful story of survival; anything that I do simply pales in comparison. This is why it is vital to protect the lines of learning for our young people. This is why I fight for what is best for the students.

In seventh grade, the Tuscarora children begin their education off the rez. They are immersed most often in American history from a Eurocentric perspective. It is imperative for our young people to have this time and space in elementary school to learn our history and the impact we had on the development of what became the United States. My dream is to have confident students who feel positive about their roots and who they are. They need to be comfortable in their own skin to be able to articulate and understand something as fundamental as the difference between Indian, Native American, First Nations, indigenous, Tuscarora, and Skaru:re. I want to provide opportunities for the young minds of not only students in our community but the district at large. I also want the students to reach a level of confidence to articulate their beliefs.

Indigenous refers to the people original to the land. My students and I discuss how we are indigenous to Turtle Island, or North America. We also discuss and learn about the indigenous people throughout the Americas.

On the north side of the Niagara River (most people refer to it as Canada), they call themselves the First Nations People. Some of our people on the south side of the river refer to themselves as Native Americans; still others might identify themselves by the specific nations that they come from, such as Hopi, Dine, or Haudenosaunee Confederacy (Iroquois). These are the waters my students must be comfortable in and be able to navigate and weave in and out of daily.

We call ourselves Skaru:re (Hemp Gatherers or People of the Shirt); most people would refer to us as Tuscarora. Each year, the students learn how, prior to contact with European people, there was no such thing as a border between what is today the United States and Canada. To us, all of North America is Turtle Island.

APPLYING HISTORY TO TODAY'S REALITIES

My dad got an old steering wheel from the local rez junkyard to do some practicing of crossing the border. This is a critical lesson for our students to be able not only to learn history, but to apply it. Students sit in a chair like it is a car. The "driver" uses the heavy old black Chevy steering wheel. The students delight in pretending to put on their seat belts while all swaying as the imaginary car takes off, turns, and pulls up to the "border." Another student mans the bridge-crossing booth, asking the typical questions of citizenship and where they are headed. Each student gets the opportunity to practice answering the questions.

Students are always encouraged to discuss with their families how they should answer at the border, especially in light of the serious nature of crossing it today. Still, to us today, we see this as North America. We see ourselves as sovereign nations that have a treaty relationship with the United States and Canada. Each year, the older students learn this history. Many of our students cross frequently to the north side of the river (Canada) for lacrosse games.

When we are stopped at the border and asked what our citizenship is, our response might be North American Indian, Native American, Iroquois, Haudenosaunee, Tuscarora, and so on. The response depends on the individual.

One year, one of my students who comes from a big lacrosse-playing family told a story in class of crossing the border into Canada with his mother. The following dialogue ensued between the crossing guard and the mother and boy:

"What are your citizenships?"
The mother responded, "American."
The boy said, "Skaru:re."
The border crossing guard said, "What?"
The boy stated again, "Skaru:re."
"What is that, French?" the border crossing guard asked.
The boy said, "No, it is Tuscarora."
The guard let them go through.

I love this story because this young man understood his history and rights, but equally important, he practiced them by responding in our indigenous language. The student also demonstrated confidence in his knowledge. The student had become empowered to define his cultural lines.

What the students need to learn is beyond the four walls of the classroom. In a world of emails, text messaging, and Twittering, we need to remember the foundation of who we are. We are the Hemp Gatherers, the sixth nation to join the Haudenosaunee Confederacy. We were one of the nations that had individuals who chose to ally with the colonies during the American Revolution and every war in which the United States has been involved. This is why I was willing to sit on an ugly, fake-leather orange chair and push into classrooms an old metal cart that I brought home one weekend to have my husband clean and paint. That was why I was willing to walk for a field trip rather than forgo it entirely. Remember as a teacher always to ask: What is in the best interest of our students?

DEVELOPING VISUAL LITERACY

"Susie, this is Eli and Lena's daughter Joanne. Why don't you take her and go play while we meet?" I remember this like it was yesterday. My parents had taken me with them while they met with the concrete man to discuss purchasing concrete for the second house they were building.

Little Susie gladly took me back to her very pink bedroom to share her toys, but rather than play with them we proceeded to jump on her two white twin beds. I remember thinking, "This is awesome!" We jumped and jumped and giggled with delight, and no one stopped us until Susie's words stopped the moment for me forever. As we jumped, Susie yelled over, "Hey, where is your horse?"

I said, "What?", thinking I didn't hear what I thought I heard. She said it again in mid-flight: "Yeah, where is your horse, and do you live in a tee-pee?" I stopped jumping. "I don't live in a teepee, and I don't have a horse." I have no memory after that moment.

This experience has led to a unit I developed in my class today about visual literacy. Reading and writing are critical to all children's success, no matter their race, ethnicity, religion, gender, or other identity markers. In today's world, all children need to be successful at reading and writing.

Visual literacy is another form of reading and writing that I know is critical to children's understanding of the world in which they live. Today, everyone is bombarded with so many visuals that our brain is actively accepting, thinking, decoding, processing, and interpreting from sunrise to sunset, yet very little is devoted to the understanding of this in the classroom. Children are faced with a myriad of visuals each and every day. Many of the images of history play a very significant role in how we view our ancestors and history in general.

What image comes to most children's minds if they are asked to draw a picture of something to do with Native Americans today? Unfortunately, just like little Susie, most students continue to have this image that Native American people ride horses and live in teepees. I have spoken before various groups of children, and often the questions are the same when they think of us. Teepees, horses, big war bonnets, and scalping continue to be the images children think of when talking about Native Americans. Cartoons perpetuate these images.

It is vital for children of all backgrounds to get a foundation of tools to begin to navigate the waters of visual images. What does that mean? For example, students learn how to view a book prior to reading it by looking at the title, illustrator, genre, and most importantly, the author. Students can investigate the authors, where they were born, and, if the book deals with an ethnicity, how qualified are they to write about this, and so on.

Visual literacy is similar in that students need to learn to have that built-in filtering screen. An example of the "screen" is: Who is the artist; from what perspective was the etching, painting, portrait, or drawing done; was the artist actually present or is it a copy of someone else's work; has the art been altered; if so, how and why?

Each year, with my fifth-grade students, I do a unit on historical images. Historical images are mostly drawings, etchings, and paintings done at the time of contact with European people. Students learn to begin to develop a filtering or questioning screen when viewing a historical indigenous image. Part of the filtering or questioning screen is: Who is the artist, what country was he or she from, was he or she an officially designated artist on a particular "expedition," or did the artist never set foot on North America and simply redraw with alterations to the original image? Many of the images schoolchildren see of Native people are done with a Eurocentric perspective. I have had students inquire as to why particular etchings look Greek.

"Mrs. Weinholtz, why are they saying 'Iroquois' in the video when they are showing a drawing of the Secotan people?" inquired Forest.

"Wow, what a great question and observation," I said to Forest. "What do you mean by that?"

"Because the video showed us, but used a picture that is not us," Forest continued.

"Yes, I am so happy you recognized how these drawing are often used to describe all 'Indians,'" I responded.

Once students become more familiar with the historic images, they begin to challenge what is used and said. They begin to develop their own questioning screen to view other materials.

Consider this example: Every year students learn about Haudenosaunee (Iroquois) pottery. Students learn about the shapes, materials, designs, usage and history. When Europeans arrived, they brought metal pots. Haudenosaunee began to trade for metal pots. All of this history contributes to building the students' visual literacy. I had a very pleasant surprise one day when my class was doing an activity with posters. I had assigned groups to put together in chronological order a stack of commercially produced posters. The posters had a variety of significant images from pre-contact to Columbus to contemporary times. Once the groups were finished, we hung the posters across our room on a clothesline. Each group chose one spokesperson to explain its poster.

When it was Zia's turn, she pointed to the pre-contact poster and said, "How can that be pre-contact?" The poster image showed the inside of an Iroquois longhouse with a woman stirring a large pot of food over the fire. I inquired of Zia why it couldn't be pre-contact when the title of the poster read "Pre-Contact" in large bold letters.

Zia responded with "How can that be pre-contact when there is a metal pot and not a clay one?"

I smiled and said, "You are correct." Zia's observation is better than any test I could give.

I have applied this visual literacy to all the images of Columbus and Pocahontas. Students are always amazed to learn that historians have no true image of Columbus because he never sat for a picture. Students are equally amazed to learn there are very few true images of Pocahontas, yet young girls are faced with images of perfection.

Literacy comes in many forms and, given the opportunity, students rise to what the teacher expects.

LOOKING TO GENERATIONS TO COME

With changes in administration and budgets, I am happy to say that I have my own classroom now. The school has been through an addition and later renovation. The outside of the school has a cradleboard design on it. A community artist studied old cradleboard patterns and colors. The cradleboard was and continues to be used by some mothers to carry their babies. When the baby is in the mother's womb, it is nourished and loved through food, thoughts, words, songs, and prayers. When the child is born, the baby is swaddled on the cradleboard just like in the womb. The cradleboard provides a straight back for the baby to have strong support. The head is protected by a brace that keeps the baby from ever bumping its head. The baby is tenderly swaddled into the cradleboard, where it learns to observe and gain in patience. Eventually, the baby grows out of the cradleboard and learns to walk, and before long, enters our school. The design on the outside of our school represents this cradleboard idea of taking the children in and nourishing them.

My classroom is the children's space. There is a story-telling area with benches and a fake fire for the cold winter months. There is a puppet theater made by some of the parents and simply loved by the students and their imagination. The cupboards are filled with things of the Earth and our culture. One of my favorite items is a set of wooden Native People family members with individual basswood tree blocks to stand them in. My mom and dad made these for the students to enjoy. The students use these like modern-day dolls. Another basket has a set of beautiful, small, and ultra-light basswood building blocks that my dad cut from a tree and sanded down. The items in the classroom that have been handmade and donated are more special than anything we could buy. We have been able to purchase paintings by local artists for permanent display in the room and throughout the school.

The beat-up, rusted gray cart that my husband saved has evolved into a beautifully painted green cart that now sits in the corner as the telephone station. The orange chair is long gone, replaced not with a slick new office chair, but a recycled chair from the 1960s at the school. The chair has wood rectangular arms with beautiful green leather covering it. Every day, I am happy to sit in this green leather chair and watch as the young people of our nation grow in confidence in their knowledge.

I am grateful to have the opportunity to teach these young people of our nation. Affording them the opportunity to learn about their roots is vital to the learning process. In an academic world of test-score rationale that demands following state standards and prescribed curriculum, teachers have not had much room or time to deviate for the students' academic advantage. Yet creating a cultural space for the students to continue to understand their history and who they are supports the learning process. Once a tree is well rooted, it will produce beautiful blossoms that bear fruit to nourish others; this is what a person's culture does for them. What better investment of academic time and effort?

We as Haudensaunee people believe you should think of the unborn faces to come and how today's decision will affect seven generations from now. I am confident in our future.

CHAPTER 9

Community Engagement Inside and Outside the Classroom

Gina E. DeShera

Gina E. DeShera was born and raised in the Santa Clara Valley in Northern California. Currently, she lives and teaches in Watsonville, California. Over the last 20 years, she has taught third grade through high school. For the last 13 years, she has been teaching middle school dance and Spanish for Spanish speakers. She is an experienced practitioner implementing multicultural education, culturally relevant, and critical pedagogy in the bilingual secondary classroom. She is also a teacher educator at San José State University.

> In theory the primary function of schools is to serve the interests of the community and its student population, in reality schools have historically functioned to serve outside interests.
>
> (Olivos, 2006, p. 45)

Many teachers will teach in communities completely unlike those in which they grew up. For example, I grew up in a largely White, Catholic, working-class neighborhood in the Santa Clara Valley in California. For the past 20-plus years, I have taught in agricultural communities of low-income Mexican and Mexican American families. For the last 13 years, I have taught at the middle school level. How can teachers like myself build connections with historically oppressed communities? How can we succeed at bringing the community and its issues into the classroom, as well as taking ourselves comfortably and authentically into the community where we teach? In this chapter, I offer teachers some insight as to how to build connections with the communities where we teach.

CHANGING MYSELF BEFORE
TRYING TO CHANGE THE WORLD

I believe the first step to building connections with marginalized communities is starting with an honest examination of your own history and family. Recognizing the privileges your family may have benefitted from due to the pigmentation of their skin or their level of education is an important step in recognizing that everyone cannot easily succeed in this society by simply "pulling themselves up by their bootstraps." My father's family emigrated from the Portuguese islands of the Azores to Kauai, where as Europeans, they were privileged enough to homestead a dairy farm. Although my family left Portugal for economic reasons, their European heritage gave them the advantage of having the opportunity to homestead land in Kauai. Contrarily, many of my students' families struggled to cross the U.S. border and have worked for years in low-paying agricultural jobs. Some are undocumented, without a process in sight for becoming legal residents or citizens. Others are highly educated in a language that is not the language of power and money, and thus, are denied access to higher-paying jobs.

My father was a typesetter for various newspapers in the San Francisco Bay area. He brought the newspaper home and read it daily. My students' parents' education levels vary from functionally illiterate to lower elementary to college level. There is a big difference in the academic support students receive in their homes according to their parents' level of formal education. My own parents spoke English and were comfortable attending parent/teacher conferences and other school events. Many of my students' parents are intimidated by a school system that is so different from their home country's and feel like their opinions may not be as valuable as the teachers'. We all have specific advantages and disadvantages in the school system according to our race, gender, socioeconomic status, and parents' education level. The challenges we face as teachers in a "foreign" community are the same challenges that our students face when they attend schools that seem "foreign" and unfriendly to them (Miser, 2006). Although it is important to acknowledge differences between your own background and your students' in order to have insight and empathy, we must be careful not to make excuses for, and expect less from, less advantaged students. A school culture of excellence with high expectations for all students is what communities want for their children, not anything less.

LIVING IN THE COMMUNITY
WHERE I TEACH

I have always lived in the communities where I teach. I choose to do this more for selfish reasons than for an altruistic motivation to connect to my students' community. I save myself a couple of hours each day by not commuting, and I use that time for my own pleasures. Yet my choice to live in the community where I teach has given me unforeseen advantages. I see my students in a variety of contexts, which makes them more human in my eyes and vice versa. For example, the other day, I saw one of my worst behavior problems fishing with his grandfather at a nearby lake. I regularly run into former students years after they were in my class. They tell me what they are doing, where they are going to college and/or working. Just today, I ran into a former student bagging groceries. He was so excited reminiscing about his performance in a professional theater in my class that he put my groceries in another lady's bag. The students remind me of memories they had in my class and make me realize which activities were truly meaningful. It is also valuable for my students to know that the community where they live includes teachers, doctors, lawyers, and other professionals.

Living in the community has facilitated my involvement in local politics and efforts toward community control. I can campaign and vote for representation on the school board, city council, and other elected positions. I read the local editorials to get a taste of the different perspectives from various individuals and groups in the community. I understand the power dynamics and political games that are played out in the community. I am able to connect with arts groups and other social and cultural activities. Most of my colleagues who don't live in this community drive home to a very distinct, mostly White, middle-to-upper-class community and only return for special school events such as open house or back-to-school night. The disconnection between school staff and community is evident and almost impossible to erase when most teachers and administrators do not live here. On the other hand, there are teachers who live in the communities where they teach and remain disconnected from their students' families, just as there are teachers who don't live in the communities where they teach who are involved and connected. Simply living near the school in which you teach is not a magic bullet that will engage you with the community, but I have found that living in the community has made it almost effortless to connect with a community that is so different from the one where I was raised. For those of you who can't possibly live in the communities where you teach, you will have to find ways to spend time participating in activities outside of the school that enable you to build relationships within the community.

RECOGNIZING THE FUNDS OF KNOWLEDGE
IN THE COMMUNITY

I live in a community that's rich in character, activism, resources, and miracles. After the local cannery was closed, causing thousands of people to lose their stable working-class wages, a vision of the Virgin de Guadalupe appeared in a tree. Today, I couldn't find a parking place in my local park where I run because there was an Aztec coming-of-age celebration for young women. The park was full of Aztec dancers in full regalia. We have mariachi singers who drive our school buses, enlightened artists who paint murals, and world-class soccer players training in local soccer fields. On Sundays, the parks are full of soccer games and extended family barbecues of *carne asada*. Aside from muralists, mariachis, and indigenous dancers, we have renowned performing arts groups of Mexican folkloric dancing and Japanese Taiko drumming. You may drive by a closed elementary school to see a group practicing a waltz for a *quinceañera* celebration. While I run in the local park, I see women walking with rosary beads and praying. Our Fourth of July parades include an army of charros on horses. We have a local and very active chapter of the Brown Berets that constantly advocates for social justice issues. If you didn't live here, and just read about this community in the newspaper, you would think this was a town of knife-wielding gangsters ready to attack anyone wearing the wrong color. You wouldn't know about the mariachis and women with rosary beads. It is important to leave ourselves open to the wisdom and understanding of the community, and to truly believe that from our students and parents will come important ways of understanding, thinking, and doing that we have not known before (Miser, 2006).

THE RESPONSIBILITY OF BEING AN INTELLECTUAL LEADER

As formally educated people working in marginalized communities, we should use our education to serve the communities where we teach, although this does not mean arrogantly believing that we are "experts" and have the answers to all issues in education. You should also be conscious not to accept a job in a marginalized community temporarily as a stepping-stone to a more desirable situation.

If a parent needs your help writing a formal letter to an educational institution, you need to make yourself available. You must be versed on parents' rights and processes for implementing change in the institution. Throughout the years, I have helped parents write letters of request for changes in placements in instructional programs. Often, the students who are born here, or have attended school in the United States since kindergarten, are tracked for years in English language development classes with no exit in sight. Many parents do not realize that with a written request they can change their son or daughter to the mainstream classes. On several occasions, I have met with parents off school grounds to help them compose letters. Parents have also asked me to translate for them at school board and School Site Council meetings. Parents have called me asking for legal advice, and I am able to connect them with local lawyers.

I am often asked my opinion about local political matters in education. At school board meetings, parents approach me to ask what exactly is going on or what they are voting on. As a teacher, I am not encouraged to interact with the parents at this level. I am always careful not to use school district resources such as copy machines, computers, and email so that I won't be accused of subordination or misuse of district resources. I have met with and helped organize parents outside of the schools, but I could never conduct these activities inside the schools. A formally educated person in a historically marginalized community should use his or her specialized expertise to serve the community without imposing opinions. I consider myself extremely privileged to have been able to obtain a degree in higher education. I recognize that many others have the same ambition, but they don't have the same opportunity. For this reason, I feel obligated to utilize my skills to help in any way that I can.

BRINGING THE COMMUNITY INTO THE CLASSROOM AND THE CLASSROOM INTO THE COMMUNITY

In the classroom, I use culturally relevant literature that brings up themes of injustice that relate to my students' families' experiences. We discuss issues of immigration, documentation, acculturation, racism, and discrimination. I develop action research projects around community issues. One year, we looked at the dropout rates of the local county high schools. Our city's high school had almost a 50% dropout rate, nearly double that of the other county schools. We looked at the numbers of students meeting university entrance requirements. Again, our local high school was far behind the others. At first, the students speculated that these must be the "bad" students who take drugs or are in gangs. The students each interviewed a friend or family member who had dropped out. They were surprised, after compiling our data, that the most frequent reason given for dropping out was to work in order to help a family survive. The students read executive summaries of educational research on conditions for Latinos in high schools and were surprised to learn that poor conditions, unprepared teachers, and segregated schools were commonplace for Latinos throughout the country. They constructed solutions such as offering alternative hours for school so students could work and attend classes. Finally, the students presented this information using PowerPoint and led a discussion on the issue of high school dropouts with the migrant parent council.

Another year, I developed a project with parents that we named "El Café Literario." A group of parents was formed that met once a week to read literature relevant to their lives and write their stories. We read *Y no se lo Tragó la Tierra* by Tomás Rivera (1996) as well as Francisco Jimenez's (2002) book *Cajas de Cartón*. Although most of the parents in this group had very little formal education, their experiences and lives have powerful stories and lessons. Their children participated with them and were proud of their parents' wisdom and excited to hear their stories. The parents made books of their published stories to share with their children and community. Copies of their books are catalogued at the school library. A year later, a local muralist collaborated with the parents and students to paint a mural of images of their stories. Each evening, for weeks, parents and their adolescent children worked on this mural with guidance from the artist. Younger brothers and sisters and even neighborhood "delinquents" joined in the activity each evening. After the mural project was finished, the "Café Literario" grew and merged with another program that aimed to decrease the digital divide and provide parents with free Internet access as well as loaner computers. Parents and their children were given instruction in basic computer use before taking home a refurbished computer. Inviting students and their families to share their knowledge is essential to students' feeling validated in the school curriculum. Parents' knowledge and experiences need to be validated in order for them to acquire ownership of their schools.

Teachers can also do fairly simple activities with parents such as keeping interactive journals between students and parents or a family member. This is a simple way to bring the families' knowledge into the classroom and open up communication. The idea is simple. Students write, using the writing workshop model, and then bring that writing home to their parents. The parents could respond to the child's writing, write something of their own, or write about what the family did over the week. During the week, the teacher writes in the journal, and the process begins again. I have to structure my time so the journals don't become too much of a burden, but the work is always fruitful and rewarding. Even the few parents who would identify themselves as "illiterate" manage to write something. Involving the families of the children we teach is the only way to have a lasting impact and to promote real school change.

The arts naturally serve as a vehicle for connecting community with school. Culturally oriented arts can help validate a collective identity, and build strength, courage, and resistance. I teach Mexican folkloric dance and spent many years traveling to Mexico to study with "maestros" from different regions. Even though I have been teaching dance and producing student performances for over 20 years, I am still surprised by how many people come to watch their family members perform and how proud they are. The connections are heartfelt. Many of my students' parents also danced in Mexico because folkloric dance is an integral part of the school curriculum there.

I realize that not every teacher can take the time to become well versed in a cultural art form. Nevertheless, teachers can lay the groundwork for students to reclaim their histories and voices through collaborative projects with community artists. At times when I have been able to acquire funding, I have collaborated with artists who represent a culture that is entirely foreign to my students and myself. In order to present a cultural dance form that I knew little about, it was essential to connect with a community artist. For a couple of years, I collaborated with a Senegalese drummer and dancer. The students' false assumptions and stereotypes about people of African descent were broken as they built a relationship with this artist. This authentic experience created a window into a culture that was so unlike their own.

Teachers who teach the arts have the means to access and validate the artistic funds of knowledge in the community. People who have cultural artistic knowledge in the community should be treasured and utilized as invaluable resources. I advocate using the artistic expertise of the families in the community to enrich our teachers, students, and curriculum. When the community is perceived to have skills, strengths, and resources that can aid children's education, the results can be phenomenal.

TRANSFORMATIVE COMMUNITY PARTICIPATION

After being both a teacher and parent in local schools, I realized how little input I had in decisions for school improvement in my son's schools as well as the school I worked in. Each year, a new school reform plan was implemented, and usually it was something I adamantly disagreed with. For example, one year, the sixth-grade students were leveled into three "tiers." I called this dumb, dumber, and dumbest. Basically, students were sorted according to their English language arts scores into different levels of remediation. The lowest level was a self-contained class that studied only language arts, math, and a period of physical education. Each year, as a new school reform plan was implemented, I considered that if it was so difficult for me to give input and possibly shape my local schools, how must it be for Spanish-speaking parents, who are unfamiliar with the dominant culture and language?

For this reason, I conducted a qualitative study at the middle school to increase critical dialogue and participation in decision making at parent council meetings among Spanish-speaking parents. A collaborative team, including parents and school staff, developed and implemented interventions that aimed to increase critical dialogue and participation from Spanish-speaking parents at parent council meetings. We implemented processes to increase communication between various school councils and improve input to school plans from the English Learner Advisory Committee and the Migrant Parent Council. Our goal was to create a sustainable partnership of school, family, and community.

We found that parents can and will contribute meaningful input on school councils if they are given the opportunity to discuss issues. Although the parent community is supposed to be the checks and balances for the school, in low-income linguistic-minority communities it is easier for school personnel to seek endorsement for their ideas rather than structure meetings to include critical dialogue about school issues. Parent groups mandated by state and federal law have long served as a confirmation for administrators to implement school reform plans rather than as participants in real dialogue. Parents are not oblivious to the injustices found in their schools, and many are willing to participate in the struggle for educational justice. As teachers, we need to participate in these conversations and struggles with families and community members. School plans need to be created *with* the community, not presented *to* the community. With guidance, parents can learn to critically review the status and performance of their own neighborhood schools and ask the right critical questions about the persistence of inequality in their schools.

STRUGGLES AND DANGERS

I discovered many dangers while working collectively with parents and the community towards changing exclusive decision-making practices to more inclusive and democratic processes. Working toward social change can be perceived as a threat to administration. Fears and accusations can be directed toward teachers who work with and help organize parent groups. I have learned that, often, working toward social justice compromises teachers in the workplace. Administrators can label teachers as adversarial sensitive to any type of criticism. Administrators have the power and authority to place you in an undesirable teaching position that you are credentialed to teach. For this reason, it is important not to work alone and to gather support from allies.

I have been accused of planting seeds, organizing the masses, manipulating opinions with my bias, and being against the school. For example, the day after a parent meeting and discussion on discrimination, the principal immediately came to my classroom during my preparation period. He was very concerned because he had heard that the parents had called him a racist.

Although a group of parents and school staff had planned and conducted this meeting, I was the only classroom teacher in the group and was perceived as the instigator. The principal had not attended the meeting but had heard from "someone" that parents had called him a racist. This was not what the parents had said or discussed. I started thinking that maybe this "someone" who told him this misinformation didn't understand Spanish well. During the parent meeting on discrimination, several students started the discussion by reading papers they wrote about their experiences with discrimination at school and in the community to small groups of parents. I showed the principal the students' papers and tried to clear up any misunderstandings. He insisted that the students' papers were not worth reading because they were biased with my (the teacher's) opinions. When I reported to him that several students wrote about teachers who prohibited them from speaking Spanish in the school, he dismissed their complaints by justifying the teachers' actions saying that they were "just trying to teach English."

Another parent meeting objective was to examine and constructively critique the instructional program for English language learners. During the stages of planning the parent meeting, an email went out that said that we were going to look at both the good and the bad in the instructional program for English learners. The principal immediately sent an email, only to me, reprimanding me for assuming that something may be wrong with the program. He stated, in no uncertain terms, "We are very proud of our program here." I realized that encouraging critical dialogue from parents around salient issues such as instructional services for language-minority students was clearly not desired. I also saw first-hand that institutions feel threatened by an informed, energized public that is attempting to change what is and what has become comfortable.

I learned quickly that it could be dangerous work for a teacher to facilitate critical discussions in parent school meetings. You put yourself in a position where you will be scrutinized for eliciting criticism. It can become uncomfortable to be cast in an adversarial light by administrators and colleagues. I believe that this is likely a reason why we don't see more teachers involved authentically with parent groups in their school communities. I know that I will never have the discussions with parents that I would like to have at parent school meetings. Some school employees will always respond to constructive criticism with a defense and explanation of why what they are doing is in the best interest of all. For this reason, I have chosen to take the most critical conversations outside the school doors, where we will not be constrained and freedom of expression will rule. Also, I have joined a variety of coalitions of parents, educators, and other community members working for educational justice in our community. Knowing that thousands of people are working beside me on these educational issues gives me the confidence to continue the struggle without fear of repercussions.

VARIOUS LEVELS OF COMMUNITY ENGAGEMENT

Teachers should engage with the community at a level that is comfortable and makes sense for them. To be effective at any level, you should first examine your own background and acknowledge privileges, differences in perspectives, as well as similarities. Even teachers with sociocultural backgrounds similar to those of the minority community where they teach should recognize that, with a college education, their own perspectives might have changed. Also, spending time outside of work hours in the community and learning the majority language is essential. Spending time in the community informally, socially, politically, or artistically is crucial to developing transformational curriculum that mirrors the community and its struggles and serves as a window to relevant issues outside of the community. The more time you spend engaging in activities in a community, the more you discover the real treasures found in any community. Utilizing those community resources in your classroom will enrich not only the curriculum you provide, but also your own learning. If your only interactions with the community are inside the school walls, you risk developing a seriously warped and inaccurate perspective.

You should not simply stand by and watch parents struggle to protect the future of their children in a school system that is often confusing, contradictory, and exploitative. You should step forward and engage in a manner that will transform both schools and society. You are an intellectual leader, having benefitted from the privilege of acquiring a college education. You should remain humble with these titles and letters after your name because they don't bestow upon you the answer to all struggles and issues. You have skills that are in short supply in a historically oppressed community, and those skills should be utilized to help. You should avoid guiding or pushing minority communities toward your own vision for a different world, but rather participate in the debates for creating this vision. The easiest and most natural way to do this is to live in the community where you teach and participate civically, not just professionally, in community matters.

PART V

Supporting Visionary Teachers

In previous chapters of this book, you have met nine incredibly creative, visionary, and hard-working classroom teachers. You have had an opportunity to learn from them how they figured out ways of engaging diverse students in meaningful academic learning and enacting culturally responsive, socially aware teaching. We hope that they have helped you to see how they keep their students as their first priority, without neglecting curriculum standards they are expected to follow. You may be thinking: "This is a lot of work; what keeps them going?" In a discussion of what keeps teachers going, Nieto (2003) commented, "Teaching is hard work, and even some of the most enthusiastic and idealistic teachers lose heart when confronted with the problems of public schools" (p. 238).

It is indeed difficult to maintain enthusiasm and creativity when resources for public schools are being cut and class sizes increased, when policies are enacted that thwart engaging teaching, and when teachers in general are routinely castigated and portrayed as inept. In a discussion of the impact of standardized approaches to teaching reading, Dudley-Marlin (2005) observed that, "Although teacher-bashing is not new, I believe this particular pastime has reached new heights in the past decade as the selling of the 'standards and accountability' model of educational reform has relied heavily on undermining the credibility of teachers and teacher educators" (p. 275). Dudley-Marlin went on to point out that the main beneficiaries of teacher-bashing are those who want to pay teachers less, and who profit from large-scale sales of "teacher-proof" curricula.

In the long run, we strongly believe that education policies in the United States must shift toward respecting and supporting the work that teachers do, and supporting processes through which novices learn to become outstanding teachers of diverse students. As Nieto (2003) points out, "Excellent teachers do not emerge full-blown at graduation" (p. 395). Teachers become excellent when they have time and support to learn in the context of practice. Ironically, test-score data help confirm this point.

Akiba and LeTendre (2009), for example, undertook a comparative study of the teaching force in the United States, Australia, and Japan because the latter two countries have been outscoring the United States on the Programme for International Student Assessment (PISA) in math and science. They found that U.S. teachers spend more time in their classrooms but have less time to prepare to teach and less time for professional development than teachers in the other two countries. Japanese teachers spend much more professional development time in one another's classrooms than do U.S. teachers, and Australian teachers spend more time collaborating in professional development than do U.S. teachers. Further, in both countries (unlike in the United States), teachers participated in developing national policies that affect teachers; in both cases, teachers' insights led to better working conditions as well as better teacher professional development.

We see teacher professional networking as essential to supporting visionary teachers and teaching, both by helping teachers hone their teaching skill, and by linking them with other professionals who offer support. Teacher networks may be informal, or formally organized through a school, school district, or university. For example, Lieberman and Pointer Mace (2008) worked with several different teacher professional networks for several years, such as the Carnegie Academy of the Scholarship of Teaching and Learning. They show how such professional learning communities, by involving teachers in collaborative inquiry into their practice, improve teaching, foster teacher leadership, and sustain teachers.

But teacher networking can offer more than sustenance, and more than professional development. For passionate visionary teachers of diverse students, teacher networks can also offer voice. For example, the network in which Nieto (2003) participated served as a powerful form of professional development, and more. In the context of talking about their work, the teachers also offered important "counternarratives" of what it means to teach:

> We rarely find words such as "love," "hope," or "anger" in current educational discourse, yet these are some of the things that kept this group of "highly qualified" and excellent teachers going. And although "social justice" and "democracy," values that also kept the teachers going, spring up in many conversations about education, they are rare in practice or policy. (p. 395)

The chapters in this last part of the book offer narratives of two different kinds of support groups for teachers. We share both examples to suggest network strategies you might seek out or develop in your own places of work. Janet Rachel Johns discusses Abriendo Caminos ("making paths"), a professional development program for secondary school teachers of emergent bilingual students (ELLs). She shares how she became involved in creating the program and what its philosophical underpinnings are, explaining that the program functions as a learning community rather than as something that is done "to" teachers. Throughout the chapter, she weaves in voices of teachers who have participated, to illustrate its impact on teachers as professionals.

Finally, a collective of teachers, known as Educators Advocating for Students, describes how and why they came together, in order to advocate for quality education for students. As you will see in their chapter, they were very concerned about how testing was driving teaching in a harmful direction. Although individual teachers usually cannot take the system on, standing collectively teachers can do so, while offering one another professional support.

CHAPTER 10

Abriendo Caminos: A Professional Learning Community for Teachers

Janet Rachel Johns

Janet Rachel Johns has been a bilingual educator since 1978, teaching grades K–8 in the Pájaro Valley Unified School District in California. For the past decade, she has worked in the area of professional development for middle and high school teachers through the program for Migrant Education, Region XI. Janet is also an active mom of a high school senior, Gabriel, and is the founder and artistic director of the Mexican Folkloric Dance Company, Esperanza del Valle. She teaches Mexican folkloric dance classes at California State University–Monterey Bay and Cabrillo College, California. She has been the choreographer for El Teatro Campesino's winter shows for the past 20 years. She is also an adjunct instructor for master's classes for bilingual certified teachers at the University of California–Santa Cruz.

Caminante, son tus huellas, el camino, y nada más;
caminante, no hay camino, se hace camino al andar.

(Traveler, there are your footprints, the path and nothing more;
traveler, there is no path, you make your path by walking.)

(Antonio Machado, in Caudet, 1987;
translation by the author)

More than 30 years ago, when I came to Watsonville, California, a majority Mexican migrant, rural community, to begin my new career as a bilingual teacher, I soon learned an important lesson, which has become a major element in the foundation of Abriendo Caminos (AC), that of establishing authentic relationships in the community in which I work. The students and families welcomed me into their homes and gatherings. The love and trust they gave me was reciprocated by my commitment to my students that went beyond the classroom walls.

Although it was hard to leave the classroom, I accepted an invitation about 10 years ago to join the Migrant Education team in the Pájaro Valley Unified School District (PVUSD) that serves Watsonville, and create a professional development program for secondary-level teachers. Migrant Education, Region XI, a federally funded program that advocates for migrant students and their families residing in the Pájaro Valley, serves more than 8,000 students, ages 3 to 21, and supports their efforts for academic success by providing health and educational services. Since the onset of my work in professional development, I have had a strong desire to eliminate the deficit labels that have been used to identify students who are learning English. I use the term *emergent bilinguals* to refer to native Spanish-speaking students of Mexican descent, as defined by García, Kleifgen, and Falchi (2008).

During my first couple of months in my new position, I tapped into a variety of resources to support me in building a professional development program. I modeled my program after the work of Pola Espinoza, the founder of Migrant Education's elementary coaching program, *Primeros Pasos* (First Steps), adapted from the work of Joyce and Showers (2002). I sent a survey to teachers districtwide, inquiring about their needs and aspirations. I met with veteran bilingual teachers, drawing on their expertise in working with adolescent emergent bilinguals using culturally relevant pedagogy. I traveled to local districts serving a similar student population, visited a number of classrooms, sat in on professional development sessions about a variety of strategies serving emergent bilinguals, and met with staff developers. Finally, Aída Walqui-van Lier, director of the Teacher Professional Development Program at WestEd, a nonprofit public research and development agency in San Francisco, provided additional resources for me to read and study to develop a program that would truly serve secondary teachers working with Mexican migrant students. Much of what I have learned from Aída has provided a foundation for the professional development program I will describe—Abriendo Caminos—in theory and practice.

Abriendo Caminos evolved from year to year as I and the teachers I work with have developed a deeper understanding of culturally relevant pedagogy. I designed Abriendo Caminos based upon my experience as a bilingual educator. Utilizing the knowledge I gained as an elementary and middle school teacher, my goal was to construct a program that would not "develop teachers," but rather establish a professional learning community of support and action for educators. I wanted to offer teachers a professional development program that is pedagogically appropriate for the advancement of adolescent emergent bilinguals; built upon the work of scholars in the fields of bilingual education, multicultural education, and critical and culturally relevant pedagogy; and grounded in the work of classroom teachers, drawing upon their knowledge and practice. AC creates a forum for teachers' individual development as they engage in critical discussion and integrate culturally relevant pedagogy into their philosophy and practice. Understanding the benefits of bridging school and home, I felt that AC should offer a space for teachers to better understand their community and recognize the importance of getting to know the student population they would be working with, believing in their students, and connecting their students' experiences to the classroom.

My passion for teaching guided my development of the AC coaching program. Teachers would participate in AC on a volunteer basis and receive supplemental pay for their time beyond contracted hours. As AC participants, classroom teachers would receive ongoing support through peer coaching to implement culturally relevant teaching of effective literacy strategies. The program I created would eventually challenge mainstream district curricular mandates, open the door to rich literature and strategies to engage students, and energize teachers to work together for social action.

The Pájaro Valley Unified School District, nestled within an agriculture-rich region of south Santa Cruz County, confronts many of the same inequities and challenges of urban school districts in its attempt to meet the academic needs of its growing emergent bilingual population. Emergent bilinguals at an intermediate or advanced level of English development are being mainstreamed into English-only classes, and teachers are expected to differentiate instruction to meet the academic needs of all students. District-initiated professional development has been largely through increased standardized approaches to instruction and curriculum, disregarding teacher expertise and the importance of sustained, ongoing professional development supported by coaching and collaborative problem solving. Teachers come to AC with the desire to add strategies to their teaching repertoire that scaffold academic content and support student learning.

The first meeting of the year is a 3-hour orientation that provides an overview of the Abriendo Caminos, its theoretical underpinnings, and the main features of the coaching component. The key strategy and dialogue meetings take place monthly, and a calendar is set for the entire school year. Throughout the year, teachers participate in professional literature study groups, reading articles by scholars in the field of bilingual education, multicultural education, and culturally relevant pedagogy. We use a number of strategies to read, and we study professional readings and debrief articles in small groups, sharing our thoughts, reflections, and insights with the whole group.

Reflecting on my experiences in developing and coordinating AC in the PVUSD, I will suggest how other educational learning communities serving a similar student population may generate a professional development approach. I asked middle and high school teachers participating in Abriendo Caminos to share their insights with me, insights that substantiated much of what I have discovered working with the program. Along with my voice, their comments are woven into the following description of AC and what I consider quality professional development for teachers of emergent bilinguals.

TEACHERS AS PROFESSIONALS

Several teachers shared that they are rarely asked what they would want to see in a professional development program, but they want to influence what it would look like and entail at their grade level districtwide. Any effective approach that serves teachers must first consider what teachers themselves deem useful in their practice. Teachers want to be treated as professionals and to have opportunities to dialogue about changes in their thinking and practice. For example, Sylvia, a middle school language arts teacher, suggests: "It has to come from teachers. . . . It doesn't work from the top-down."

A 20-year veteran bilingual middle school teacher, Catrina acknowledges many reasons why she chose to participate in AC professional development: "Being paid for my time after contracted hours is something that said to me, 'This is a program that understands the labor conditions of a teacher.' Most professional development programs purport to be the magic bullet, and as a good teacher you should just attend them from your burning desire to better your teaching."

Language arts teacher Elena sums up her feelings: "I define this [AC] as . . . constant growth; you never stop growing. I just feel it's invaluable to get together with other professionals."

Teachers acknowledge the importance of being part of a learning community and collaborating with other teachers. Teachers come to AC because they know that they will be treated like professionals and have a direct influence on their own learning.

GROUNDED IN TEACHERS' PRACTICE

I often hear teachers complain that outside learning experiences are too far removed from the classroom to be meaningful to their day-to-day work.

As Catrina put it, "The district only offers textbook training and canned professional development programs . . . aimed at raising test scores and maintaining status quo. . . . Most teachers hate having to leave their classes and go to a district-mandated professional development." Teachers feel invalidated by traditional forms of top-down professional development that present one size fits all approaches and rely on outside experts who "supposedly" supply teachers with the knowledge they lack, without acknowledging their experiences, skills, and perspectives.

In contrast, the AC approach is grounded in the needs and perspectives of teachers and students. In order for professional development to be meaningful, approaches like AC ground teachers' learning experiences in their own practice, with learning taking place in individual teachers' classrooms and during sessions outside the classroom that are focused on instructional practices and pedagogy. AC teachers' learning is connected with their ongoing practice, which seems to influence and support their teaching in meaningful ways. In contrast to deficit models of teacher learning, professional development approaches should build upon the experiences, skills, and knowledge of each teacher and, in turn, create opportunities for teachers to share their knowledge and experiences with one another.

SAFE SPACE FOR TEACHERS

Teachers feel that there is an absence of intellectual discussion in district-provided professional development and a lack of time and space for teachers to ponder what they consider key topics in teaching and learning. Abriendo Caminos provides a safe space for teachers to collaborate with one another and discuss critical issues, such as district policy mandates, bilingualism, tracking, and critical and culturally relevant pedagogy. At AC, teachers feel that their intellectual capacity to make decisions for their own professional growth is honored. As Catrina put it: "AC has provided us the 'third space' . . . to dialogue, debate, and be critical of educational policy away from the ears of our administrators." Teachers value the time and space to further develop as critical and social justice educators and ponder critical issues together. They also value having a safe space to talk with colleagues and challenge the current standardized approaches to accountability and instruction. At AC dialogue meetings, teachers have opportunities to discuss the prescriptive nature of test-driven curriculum and share their frustrations and possible solutions to reverse a system that is academically limiting for adolescent emergent bilinguals.

Behind AC's closed doors, teachers feel safe to discuss culturally relevant pedagogy and creative resistance to textbook teaching, and to gain the support of their peers. Although teachers have struggled to teach emergent bilingual students within the context of mandated scripted programs and reading intervention programs, there is an underlying and understated resistance on the part of these teachers that has enabled them to use culturally relevant pedagogical practices in their classrooms. Marisol, a newcomer middle school teacher, explains: "I use my creative resistance . . . to utilize their language, their experiences, their histories, and ideas to communicate a valid source of history. . . . This is a pedagogy that de-centers the oppression and empowers the oppressed, while still making it academic, challenging and enriching." AC supports teachers as they negotiate and resist the policy context. At AC, teachers create an environment to explore, challenge, support, or refine their perceptions or practices on critical and culturally relevant pedagogy through their participation.

CULTURALLY RELEVANT PEDAGOGY

At AC, our definition of culturally relevant pedagogy is multifaceted. Culturally relevant teaching recognizes bilingualism and the importance of the home language for linguistic and academic development. It acknowledges and validates the funds of knowledge (González, Moll, & Amanti, 2005) that each student brings to school and connects to their lived experiences and communities. As teachers' understanding of culturally relevant pedagogy deepens, they transform in their thinking and practice and learn how to teach and advocate for students who are culturally and linguistically diverse. Teachers share how culturally relevant pedagogy helps transform their pedagogical perspectives and practices. Knowing that the mandated curriculum in the secondary classroom presents one perspective—that of the textbook authors—AC offers participating teachers additional resources, such as the *Rethinking Schools* publications, that provide perspectives and ideas for curriculum that validates our students' experiences and language. Teachers teach the standards, but resist the mainstream canons of truth, offering students additional perspectives and experiences. For example, a high school English teacher uses a *Rethinking Schools* publication on NAFTA to incite students to write persuasive essays on real issues that affect their lives.

Offering the latest research, AC focuses on the positive effects of additive bilingual education and the continued development of the home language. Teaching in communities like Pájaro, where the majority of emergent bilinguals come from Spanish-speaking homes, teachers feel supported at AC as they address language issues confronting adolescent emergent bilinguals in the secondary classroom. For example, as Carina shares, "When students work in their primary language, they suddenly seem brilliant rather than remedial." Marisol agrees: "Language is power, and when schools try to narrow a classroom language to that of only English, we tell our students that they have none when they chose to speak their own." I have learned that teachers require multiple opportunities to challenge and enhance their perspectives on bilingual education, through professional readings, focus groups, dialogue meetings, observations, and model lessons in the classroom. Often, when teachers do not live in the same communities where they teach, they need time and space to explore issues such as bilingualism and the use of primary language in the classroom.

I frame our work as educators through a critical and culturally relevant lens. Because teachers come to the program at different stages in their development regarding culturally relevant pedagogy, I find it necessary to work with each teacher individually. Through professional readings, reflective conversations, and classroom coaching, I provide teachers with multiple opportunities to challenge their views and practice on culturally relevant pedagogy, including the use of primary language for their students' development of literacy and second-language acquisition, the strategies they use to support students in their learning, as well as the content being used.

EFFECTIVE TEACHING AND LEARNING: AC STRATEGIES

Teachers come to AC to be a part of a community of learners for quality teaching and learning. An important personal goal of mine is to support the teachers in the preparation of curriculum and materials. I support every teacher in my program on an individual basis and tailor instruction to meet their students' needs. The strategies and curriculum that I introduce and implement vary from teacher to teacher. No two teachers or classrooms are alike.

However, some common threads run through them because they are tailored to the specific needs of emergent bilinguals. I develop lessons *into, through,* and *beyond* to facilitate students' understanding of text. *Into* activities and strategies prepare the learner before reading, *through* activities and strategies guide learners collaboratively through the text, and *beyond* activities and strategies extend the learner's knowledge and vocabulary. Over the course of a decade, I have developed an archive of curriculum available to every teacher in the program that utilizes the following key strategies:

- Specially Designed Academic Instruction in English (SDAIE) is the teaching of grade-level subject matter in English for students who have reached an intermediate level of English proficiency. AC designs lessons using the scaffolds developed by Walqui (2006) to prepare learners before reading, guide them through the text, and extend their understanding once they have read. For example, the scaffold of modeling entails providing students with a clear example of a product they are expected to produce.

- Reciprocal Teaching is an interactive reading strategy for a small group of four to six students, structured by the use of four reading comprehension strategies: questioning, clarifying, summarizing, and predicting. Students alternate taking on the role of the teacher and directing the dialogue with their peers.
- Interactive Journals provide students with a place to practice their writing through self-selected topics. Students have personal and direct access to their teachers who respond to journal entries. Learning Logs are content-driven and teacher-directed, providing students with a place to reflect on what they know, what they don't know and want to learn, and how it relates to their lives.
- Thematic Instruction transforms a unit of study into eight learning centers that meet the content standards. Students work in cooperative groups and are self-directed to complete the work in each center while the teacher serves as facilitator. Centers are academically challenging, yet culturally relevant to the students.
- Literature Studies create opportunities for students to explore literature and to engage in literature response in a small-group setting. Working in small groups, students chose a piece of literature from a teacher-selected group of books. They guide themselves through a structured process to anticipate, read, discuss, and participate in a variety of extension activities to demonstrate their understanding. Clear directions are posted in each literature study center. Groups self-evaluate their process on a daily basis.
- Writers' Workshop offers students writing options available to real authors. They choose their topics and learn the process of writing. They draft, revise, and edit their writing with their teacher and peers.

Each key strategy contains a plethora of activities and strategies to teach important concepts and skills. I create lessons that teach the targeted strategies through the specific content of the classroom, be it economics or Earth science. For example, students are introduced to the concept of earthquakes with a Directed Seeing Thinking Activity that grabs students' attention to make predictions of a hidden picture, which the teacher reveals one piece at a time. The Anticipatory Guide engages the readers by activating their background knowledge about earthquakes by asking if they agree or disagree with five statements. Find the Meaning is an activity to introduce key science vocabulary in the text as students collaborate with one another.

Directed Reading with Numbered Heads guides students to read the text collaboratively in small groups, with time to negotiate meaning and learn from one another.

Elena explains what she gains by participating in AC: "I feel that it has changed a lot of the ways that I teach. I do a lot more interactive teaching with the students. . . . Students do a lot more group work. The techniques are wonderful, they're invaluable, and I would recommend every teacher, especially a new teacher, participate in a program like Abriendo Caminos."

REFLECTIVE PRACTICE THROUGH COACHING

The key to changing teacher practice is when teachers are shown and able to practice new strategies and sustain growth through ongoing coaching. The AC coaching cycle is comprehensive, targeting teachers' specific needs, as they implement new strategies and make them part of their instructional repertoire. A full cycle begins with a strategy session after school where teachers learn and practice the new strategy. I then create lessons that use the strategies and activities targeted. I model the lesson in the classroom with the students while the teacher observes and coaches. We reflect on the lesson together, recognizing what went well and areas for improvement or change. The cycle continues as teachers invite me back to the classroom to serve as their coach and observe them using the strategy with their students (Joyce & Showers, 2002). We interchange the roles of coach and teacher continuously. When I, as the coach, model a lesson in the classroom with the students and take on the role of the teacher, the classroom teacher becomes my coach.

Teachers recognize the coaching cycle to be the most helpful component of AC when it comes to transforming their practice and supporting the implementation of effective strategies into their teaching repertoire. Daphne, a teacher of language arts, English language development, and social studies, clarifies: "I like the idea of . . . having a mentor . . . to model the different strategies and answer questions, too." It is important for teachers to commit to the full coaching cycle and attend monthly afterschool meetings in order to transform practice and pedagogy.

Before I model a specific strategy with the students in the classroom, I meet with each teacher at her or his site for planning. We look at the standards and decide on the chapter, lesson, or theme that I will be teaching using the AC strategy. At that time, I get a sense of the classroom, how the furniture is arranged, and the management strategies used during instruction. The majority of AC strategies require that students work in small groups, so I inform the teachers that I may have to change the furniture during the model lesson. I borrow any necessary texts to prepare my lesson and use the textbook as a base. I usually go beyond the text to create lessons *into, through,* and *beyond* and integrate the six instructional scaffolds—modeling, bridging, contextualization, building schema, representing text, and developing metacognition—that Aída Walqui (2006) developed to use with emergent bilinguals. Model lessons usually last 2 to 4 hours, but I create lesson plans for a week. I prepare all materials, including overheads, instructional charts, student learning logs, and guides.

During the demonstration lesson with the students, teachers act as my peer coach and use the AC observation sheet to record teacher and student behaviors. Each lesson is followed by a reflection meeting with the classroom teacher. We use a reflection sheet to guide our conversation about the lesson observed. Reflections are elicited from the classroom teacher and are not given as feedback by the coach. Whether I'm modeling or observing a lesson, the classroom teacher must direct this conversation. The following questions guide our reflections and thoughts on the lesson:

- What worked?
- How could you tell?
- What were the challenges/obstacles?
- How would you change the lesson?
- What's next?

Once the classroom teacher has had time to practice the strategy with his or her students, I am invited to observe the teacher in action. We often meet to plan the lesson collaboratively, and the teacher lets me know when to come in and what to focus on. I use the same observation sheets that the teacher used during the demonstration lesson that I modeled earlier that month, and afterward, the teacher and I participate in a reflection meeting. Sylvia explains: "I really like the Abriendo Caminos model . . . the whole cycle of having someone show it to you . . . then you show it to them, then you keep doing that cycle."

ABRIENDO CAMINOS LEVEL II

Teachers may participate in ACI from 1 to 3 years with full coaching support. I created another level for AC teachers who had participated in the program for more than 3 years and were ready to take on new and different challenges in their growth as teacher leaders. Initially, ACII was created to support teachers for an unlimited amount of time to develop their skills as peer coaches at the middle and high school sites. Those teachers who demonstrated a strong knowledge of AC strategies and wanted to continue to develop and refine their practice as culturally relevant educators were invited to participate in ACII. During the early years of the program, my goal was to have at least one ACII peer coach at every secondary site in the district. These teachers would serve as peer coaches to other teachers at their schools and, in particular, to ACI teachers. ACII meetings would provide time for these teachers to develop coaching skills and to discuss the successes and challenges they were experiencing in their work with ACI teachers.

ACII teachers find creative ways to support and coach teachers at their site since they are all full-time classroom teachers. They offer their classrooms as demonstration classrooms where colleagues can observe them using AC strategies and lessons with their students. Some find time to plan curriculum together and discuss critical issues. Very few have time to actually observe or model a lesson in a colleague's classroom, due to their teaching load. ACII teachers often co-present with me at ACI key strategy meetings and share their experiences with ACI teachers.

ACII teachers have been critical allies for the AC program. When discussions ensue at AC meetings involving topics such as race, social justice, political activism, and bilingual education, the ACII teachers offer their voices and experiences to guide the discussion. I depend on the expertise of ACII to help support ACI teachers to open their hearts and minds and challenge their perspectives and practices.

We also meet separately from the ACI teachers as a professional learning community and focus on current educational issues and policies challenging equitable education for emergent bilinguals. ACII teachers request that the latest research be a part of the discussion. Each year, we read one book on an education-related topic and a number of articles, using Literature Studies as a strategy to read and review the text as a group and share our insights with our colleagues. Cristina, a veteran bilingual teacher, sums it up: "I have been able to get from ACII what I miss from being a university student, which is true discussion and critical analysis . . . what it means to be a teacher in my community."

WHAT I HAVE LEARNED

If the saying is true that education is political, then it is also true that we are not neutral in our philosophy and practice as teachers. As a teacher educator, I have learned that it is better for teachers to understand my stance on bilingual education and multicultural education than for me to pretend to be neutral. Although AC is framed under a multicultural lens, it is open to all teachers who wish to participate, as long as they work with emergent bilinguals. I have worked with both like-minded educators and those who may not agree with my philosophies. Often, the necessity to learn new strategies in working with this student population draws unlikely candidates to my program. I work hardest with these teachers, modeling lessons in their classrooms and developing curriculum to serve their students. They usually give me their most challenging class to work with. I do whatever I can to make sure that the lesson is successful and take the time to debrief and reflect on the results. It is the relationship that we develop through the classroom work and reflective conversations that open minds and hearts toward a willingness to move their practice and educational philosophy forward. They begin to talk about the use of primary language in the classroom or collaborative strategies that encourage them to move their students into groups.

It was a difficult decision to leave my position as a middle school classroom teacher to work in professional development. After more than a decade of providing professional development for middle and high school teachers, I still consider myself a classroom teacher and am continuously refining my skills directly in the classroom with students. Teachers do not want to be "professionally developed." Teachers want to be a part of the conversation, treated as equals, and work with a coach who is actually working with them, side by side in their classrooms modeling lessons with the students and not just observing and giving advice. By providing a forum for teachers, I have discovered the power of teachers developing themselves and one another, and my role as a guide to support them in their teaching and learning journeys.

Because the AC program represents one of the few professional development approaches in our district that draws on critical and progressive philosophies, it has been a challenge to keep the program safe from district policy mandates and top-down professional development. In fact, many teachers are drawn to AC to develop creative resistance to policies and practices that thwart culturally relevant teaching. Professional development programs, like AC, need a safe place to exist and flourish. For over a decade, the director of Migrant Education has committed resources, personnel, and time for Abriendo Caminos to ensure the programs' sustainability and survival. By housing the program within the walls of the federally funded Migrant Education program, AC is kept safe from the district's political environment, policy mandates, and transitory trends in professional development.

Programs like AC require a full-time coordinator/coach to oversee the program and support the teachers and teacher coaches at individual school sites. That person must be committed to continuously honing his or her own practice and skills by working directly in the classroom with students. I can't expect a teacher to believe that a strategy will work with his or her own students if I can't demonstrate the strategy first-hand with the students. Working directly in the classroom with teachers and their students builds trust, which is necessary to transform perspectives and practices. As the AC coach, I put relationships with teachers first and foremost before all other components of the program, which parallels the most productive kind of relationship between teachers and their students. In addition, a coach must have the intellectual knowledge to guide and support teachers as they add new instructional strategies to their repertoire. This comes with years of practice and experience in the classroom and the desire to continue to develop a knowledge base of current research and pedagogy. Finally, a coach with a lens for culturally relevant pedagogy and the intellectual knowledge and experience in working with culturally and linguistically diverse student populations will better serve teachers of these students.

Linda Christensen (2009), author and member of *Rethinking Schools* publications, shares: "Teaching for joy and justice isn't an individual endeavor. We can't do this work alone" (p. 9). Working within a critical collaborative community supports teachers in developing culturally relevant pedagogy and enables us to create pedagogically sound learning environments for students that draw on their language, culture, and experiences.

CHAPTER 11

The Power of Networking: Teachers Advocating for Change

Members of Educators Advocating for Students:
Eileen Clark Nagaoka, Theresa Gilbert, Elizabeth Hiltz,
Teri Marchese, Lucinda Pease-Alvarez, Rita Ramirez,
Sarah Ringler, Franciscio Rodriguez, and Lucia Villareal

Educators Advocating for Students is a grassroots teacher group committed to developing a collective, local response to the current educational policy. The membership includes teachers, teacher educators, and researchers who came together with common concerns. Their varied teaching experiences in elementary, middle, and high schools, including individuals with 5–35 years in the field, both bilingual and English-speaking, have helped them take action and network as advocates for their students.

Most of the members of Educators Advocating for Students (EAS) work in schools in a district serving 19,000 students from two very different communities. The majority of residents in one community are White and middle- or upper-class. In contrast, the majority of residents in the other are poor, working-class, and of Mexican origin. In general, the schools in our district are segregated: Most White students attend schools in the eastern region of the district, and the majority of Latino students, many of whom are officially designated as English learners, attend schools in the western region.

In this chapter, we will describe our experiences advocating for change that would enhance the educational and life opportunities of our students and their families. Much of our work has focused on how to change federal, state, and district policies that have resulted in one size fits all approaches to teaching and assessing English language learners. After describing this environment and how it has affected us professionally, we will tell our story, highlighting our efforts to change testing and assessment policies and what we have learned from our involvement in EAS as individuals and a collective.

WORKING IN A CLIMATE OF COMPLIANCE

The 2002 reauthorization of the Elementary and Secondary Education Act, commonly known as NCLB, has had a profound impact on the lives of teachers and students in our state and district. Under NCLB, grades 3–8 are required to test 95% of student subgroups, including students identified as English learners, on a yearly basis in the areas of mathematics, English language arts, and science. In California, testing begins in the second grade and, for the most part, is done in English, regardless of the language proficiency of the students being tested. Schools with student subgroups that fail to meet yearly targets in a specific subject area are declared program improvement (PI) schools and subject to sanctions, which include providing parents with the option of transferring their children to another school, restructuring the curriculum and its "delivery" to entail the use of prepackaged curricula, offering supplemental tutoring, and, in the case of schools that repeatedly fail to meet yearly state-imposed benchmarks, reassigning staff and school closure.

Most of us teach in schools that have been declared PI, and our entire district has been declared a PI district. Teachers who work in PI schools or who work in classrooms that serve mostly English learners face a challenging and oppressive work environment. In the following reflection, written in the summer of 2007, Marcela provides her perspective on the policy environment that teachers were facing around the time EAS was established. We consider Marcela's perspective to be particularly noteworthy, given her standing as a veteran teacher with more than 30 years working in our district and her history of activism.

> What has it been like to teach in a program improvement school? To date, this question has not been asked of us teachers in a format in which we can be open and specific. Any input we are asked to give has been redirected, muffled, and muted such that, through the years, most teachers voicing concerns regarding district and site educational practices have been silenced.
>
> Before I continue with a teacher's view, I want to propose that a more important question is, "What is it like to be a learner in a PI school in our district?" This question is very important because it is the student who is the one at the receiving end of all the decisions made and changes brought about due to the state and district interpretations of No Child Left Behind. The impact has fallen squarely on the learner's shoulders. The words commonly used to describe these students are *underachieving, underperforming*, and *challenged*. Decision makers treat the learner in a PI school as less than whole. They are deemed to be less than whole because they are

not up to par due to scores that do not contribute positively enough to the AYP (annual yearly progress) of a school.

The life of a teacher in a PI school is one where we are forced to keep silent as we watch these punitive "test and punish" state and district policies take their toll on our students. Our professional lives are controlled so that we are "encouraged" to be no more than publisher-company classroom clerks following the district-adopted reading and writing programs. We are monitored by groups of administrators and others who come to our classrooms to check up on what is on the walls, chart stands, and boards to see if they indicate a strict "robot-like" adherence to the adopted program. We are monitored to check if we are giving the many monthly tests and if we input the results into the district data systems.

We know that to follow those kinds of educational practices is to perform in the realm of professional bankruptcy. Yet, questioning is not accepted. Those who voice concerns are labeled "complainers" at best, and at worst, are called in and accused of not being a "team player" and told to "change their attitude." For many years, even our union leadership was part of the monitoring group that "shamed and blamed" us.

We teachers in PI schools have very high academic expectations for our students, and we welcome the accountability that goes with that. We welcome change and improvement. But what need to be in place are state and district policies that encourage real teaching and learning, along with assessments that don't just encourage skills-focused lessons that teach to the test. We need to move away from what the National Center for Fair and Open Testing (2007) labels as testing that "encourages a narrowed curriculum, outdated methods of instruction, and harmful practices such as retention in grade and tracking." We PI teachers want instructional and assessment practices that truly are conducive to real and meaningful learning along with strong skills in all areas of the curriculum. Isn't this what every student needs and parents and the community want?

As Marcela describes, we are required to fully implement prepackaged curriculum with "fidelity" and without question. We are targets of surveillance on the part of district administrators who periodically monitor whether or not we are complying with curricular requirements by conducting 5- to 10-minute visits in our classrooms. During these visits or "walk-throughs," a committee of administrators enters our classrooms, takes notes, asks questions of students, and sometimes interrupts our instruction. When providing feedback after "walk-throughs," district administrators seldom meet with us. Instead, they report their "findings" to principals.

At the time Marcela wrote her reflection, teachers had no official venue for expressing their concerns about policies to district administrators. Indeed, those of us who tried were told that there was nothing we could do and that any effort to resist policies could result in a formal written reprimand that would be placed in our personnel file. When we raised questions about policies, we were told that to not fully comply with them meant that we were not doing our job and/or that we didn't care about whether or not our students learned. Needless to say, many teachers working in our district were demoralized, angry, and fearful. For many, these feelings have endured.

THE BEGINNING OF EAS

We trace our beginnings to October 2007, when a student teacher told her education professor, Cindy, that Jan, her cooperating teacher, would like to talk with Cindy. In an email, Jan told Cindy about her plan to supplement the required language arts curriculum by providing her students with opportunities to read and discuss novels. Cindy discussed the situation with Amy, one of the student teacher supervisors, who suggested that she and Cindy meet with Jan to discuss her plan.

Over coffee, Jan told Amy and Cindy that both her principal and the assistant superintendent had rejected her plan. In addition, she shared a number of other concerns regarding district policies, including the district mandate requiring that students be assessed in reading and writing using tests that provided very limited information about children's abilities and needs, her general concern regarding the lack of voice teachers had when it came to instructional decision making, and a growing lack of communication and trust between teachers and school and district administrators. After Cindy and Amy mentioned that they had talked with other teachers in the district who shared Jan's concerns, they all agreed that it would be good to get together with these teachers to share their issues and possibly brainstorm ways to address them. After deciding on a date for an informal gathering at Cindy's house, Jan and Amy invited teachers they knew who were concerned about similar policies to this initial meeting.

In addition to Jan, Amy, and Cindy, five teachers from three different school sites met at Cindy's house in early December. Immediately, their discussion turned to district assessment policies. Teachers raised concerns about utilizing valuable instructional time to administer and prepare children, who were not yet English proficient, for the district-mandated tests and assessments that had been developed for native English speakers. Melinda, a second-grade teacher, shared a letter she had given district administrators who had visited her classroom. In this letter, she described several concerns she had about the district's testing and assessment policies, including the hours spent on testing and test preparation that provided her with little useful information about how to meet her students' academic needs. Administrators never communicated with Melinda about the contents of her letter.

More than 25 teachers attended the next meeting, held in late January 2008. During that meeting, group members shared issues and set priorities for action focused on assessment and testing policies. These actions included developing a position statement outlining our concerns, obtaining teacher signatures endorsing the statement, sending the statement to local newspapers, and having teachers appear on a local TV program to discuss their concerns regarding district policies. During the meeting, Anne and the new president of the local affiliate of the teachers' union invited the group to become part of the Working Conditions Subcommittee of the union.

With the exception of summers, the group has met at least once a month since its initial meeting. Although the greatest number of teachers turned out for our January 2008 meeting, a core group of between 8 and 10 teachers have been attending most meetings. Many other teachers have, to various degrees, maintained contact with the group via a password-protected Web site that was established in the spring of 2008. The group also decided to give itself a name and adopt the following mission statement:

> The EAS Coalition is a group of teachers committed to equity, diversity, student achievement, and community involvement. Central to the vision and mission of the group are concerns about the effects of the accountability movement, including the misuse of time and resources for standardized testing, diminishment of formative assessments to guide and direct assessment, reduction of time for a balanced education (including the teaching of science, social studies, art, and music) as well as the positioning of textbooks as curriculum rather than teachers' resources. The group is fundamentally opposed to the recently narrowed conception of schooling and the lack of time, attention, and resources allocated to children's social-emotional development, and the fostering of their cultural and linguistic identity. We support the reinstatement of the teacher as an active and vital member of instructional decision making and believe that teachers should be valued as professional stewards of the educational process. Our mission includes providing a forum for support, educating the community, and organizing advocacy efforts on behalf of our students and their families

EAS AS A VENUE FOR COLLECTIVE ACTION

During our meetings, we have discussed a range of issues that impact our lives as teachers and the lives of our students and their families. Beginning with our first meeting, the majority of our collective efforts have focused on changing district and state testing and assessment policies. Here, we focus in greater detail on these efforts.

Drawing on similar points to those that Melinda raised in her letter about district testing policies, we devoted several meetings in winter of 2008 to crafting the following statement.

Program Improvement?

Students across our district are currently losing over 100 hours of instructional time, 50 days of prime reading and writing instruction, due to mandated tests. Tack onto that another 30-plus hours lost for test preparation and practice. Very little of this actually helps students improve their skills, nor does it give their teachers much useful information. Furthermore, teachers are required to administer these tests to all their students, even those who are learning English as a second language and some special needs children.

All across the district, schools are being labeled "Program Improvement Schools." This means they have joined the growing ranks of California schools that have not yet met state or federal standardized test benchmark scores. In our district, improving a school program has come to mean testing students until their eyes glaze over. Students are losing out on social studies, science, and art so that they can be "prepared" for all of the language arts and math testing. They are being subjected to a repeating tsunami of over 100 hours of testing that hits them in waves every 3 to 6 weeks throughout the year. This results in teachers spending hours of valuable planning time correcting, analyzing, and entering data based on these tests.

District assessment decisions are final and mandated by personnel who are far removed from the classroom. Teachers who interact with students on a daily basis no longer have a voice in how to teach or assess the students they work with and know well. Moreover, many questions and concerns teachers direct to district administration and consultants, about testing policies and mandates, go unanswered.

As teachers, we believe that instructional time is extremely precious and needs to be carefully guarded, especially when students are working so hard to reach grade-level standards. We fully understand the value of assessment that informs teaching and enhances learning. Teachers are asking to get back to the kind of useful, diagnostic assessments that actually help them to know what students have learned, what they need to review, and what to teach next.

The reality in the district is that teachers have few opportunities to contribute to decisions related to the use and implementation of these mandated tests. District administration has taken the job of educating our kids out of the hands of knowledgeable teachers and hired it out to "consultants" who don't work with kids, and whose "program improvements" are themselves untested and whose results are unproven.

Please help stop this madness. Express your concern over instructional time that has been lost to demoralizing, repetitive testing, and ask that teachers once again be included in decisions about how to assess the kids they know best. Contact your teachers, principals, school site council, school board representatives, or send letters to the editor with your input. Support the children of our district and their teachers.

In addition to spending hours composing and revising this statement, union representatives shared the statement at their site meetings where they told their colleagues that they could sign the statement without revealing their identity using terms such as "non-tenured teacher #1." Once 200 teachers signed the statement, we asked reporters from three different local newspapers to publish it. Over the course of a 3- to 4-week period in March, the statement was published in each newspaper, including a Spanish version of the statement in a Spanish-medium newspaper that is read by many of our students' family members.

We also engaged in other actions focused on district and state testing policies. Several members were interviewed about their views on testing and other issues in a follow-up article that was published shortly after the letter. Four members of EAS also participated in a panel that was featured on a local community TV program focused on testing. In late September 2008, two members read the statement to a group of parents participating in a monthly community gathering. Afterward, they answered questions from parents. We handed out postcards describing our concerns about testing, which were printed in English and Spanish, to parents and community members who were willing to sign them and send them to their state representative. In December, Sarah drew on the statement to draft a resolution calling for a testing moratorium that would be part of a nationwide campaign supported by the American Federation of Teachers. After two members of our group helped her revise the letter, she shared the resolution at a districtwide meeting of the union. The local union membership authorized the resolution via a ballot that was disseminated to every teacher in the district. After local teachers voted in favor of the resolution, Sarah presented it at the statewide meeting of the union, where it was voted on and approved.

Our desire for teacher input into district policies related to testing was also reflected in the 2008–9 contract negotiations, as evident in the following clause that appeared in the final version of the contract:

> The District acknowledges the need to review the total number of assessments being administered throughout the District and to support only those assessments determined to be effective and necessary as a Program Improvement District. The District shall seek the input of the union's assessment committee on this topic.

Shortly after the contract was negotiated, the union president asked that three members of EAS join the district's assessment committee, which is charged with providing an evaluation of the tests and other assessments that the district requires. Although the district has not yet convened this committee, the union continues to advocate for it. The union president and the three members of EAS who will serve on the assessment committee have been involved in a series of meetings with the superintendent about this and other issues.

EAS AS A VENUE FOR PROFESSIONAL GROWTH

In addition to being a venue for collective action, our involvement in EAS has contributed to our professional growth and well-being. By participating in EAS, we have grown as both leaders and educators. The following reflection by Maureen underscores the impact EAS has on the professional development of a new teacher:

> I started coming to the EAS meetings with a couple colleagues of mine during my first year with the district. We all taught 2nd grade and had many conversations about the frequency of [required] testing and preparing students for these tests. We had learned that there was a group of concerned educators discussing the impact of the [testing] and attempting to bridge the gap between university theories and practices and the school sites dealing with the pressures of testing. My colleagues and I arrived to a house full of educators sharing stories, sympathizing with one another and brainstorming a plan. At first, the group met secretively. Conversations were confidential, names withheld. We didn't tell anyone at our site about our monthly meetings. The four of us would continue to attend meetings during the first 6 months.

Attending these meetings became the foundation for my future involvement at my site and within the district. Still, not being a tenured teacher has made me nervous to participate. I prefer to take on anonymous roles to help our group educate others in our community. I set up an Internet forum for our group members to discuss and share ideas.

In November of the second year, while attending an EAS meeting, the union president asked for a last-minute volunteer to represent the union on a tour of another school district. I was going on this "field trip" with several administrators from other district schools, my district administrators, and superintendents. I was the only classroom teacher in attendance. I knew that my role was to be the eyes and the ears for teachers. The field trip's purpose was to learn how this district had improved their test scores, built professional learning communities, analyzed data, written common assessments, and, in turn, got their schools out of program improvement sanctions. My role representing union teachers was intimidating. Conversations with these administrators were scary. But I knew that EAS members would be supportive of me and were excited that one of our members was there to represent our concerns and beliefs.

This experience propelled me into future leadership roles at my school and at the district level. Our EAS meetings offer me a chance to share what I learn and learn from other members. During our meetings, I'm able to discuss new ideas with a professional group of critical thinking educators. I like the insight and support that I get from our monthly EAS meetings, it encourages me to look at issues from new and different perspectives that may have been overlooked by the presenters or district employees.

Most important, EAS has impacted my teaching. I do not feel intimidated by others' ideas that I should teach to the test. I have used my voice in team meetings to set the tone that we no longer need to teach to each individual test. I also began to teach more in Spanish, whereas my grade level (due to the pressures of state standardized exams) had begun to transition bilingual 2nd-grade students at the mid-year, rather than in 3rd grade as other Early Exit Programs do.

I am now the only teacher from my site who attends the meetings. I always leave EAS meetings feeling invigorated, educated, knowledgeable, and ready to continue to fight the good fight.

LESSONS LEARNED ABOUT COLLECTIVE ACTION

When responding to top-down policy mandates that we think are harmful to students, we have tended to take the approach of working within the system by trying to communicate our concerns about district policies to administrators. We have also pushed against the system to make sure that our voice is heard on those occasions when administrators have not responded to our concerns, not provided us a place at the policymaking table, or persisted in their enforcement of policies that do harm to children, families, and teachers. This was most evident in our collective response to district and statewide testing initiatives.

In working to make sure that teachers have input in the policymaking process, we have learned a number of important lessons. Perhaps first and foremost, we have learned the value of collaborative working relationships. This is evident in the way we mobilize our collective knowledge and resources. When building on points from Melinda's original letter about assessment and testing policies, we drew on the knowledge, commitments, and writing abilities of our membership. During EAS meetings, we also mobilized our collective knowledge in ways that inform individual as well as collective action. In the following reflection, Anne describes how this has enabled her to be more effective when advocating for students and families at her school site:

> As a college student, teacher, parent, and community member, I've long been active in local and national political movements. However, the demands of the No Child Left Behind legislation were at once so sweeping, so powerful, and cloaked in such confusing language, that the avenue for addressing its problems was not clear. Upon its passage, I was left feeling more isolated and misunderstood than ever, feeling my way in the dark through new territory.
>
> Being a member of EAS has brought light to this process. Having colleagues from the same district, especially colleagues who were also from schools in "program improvement" status, come together to share frustrations with the mandates of NCLB and Reading First brought huge relief. As one of the few veteran teachers at my site, I am one of a very small group who tests the limits of the restrictions imposed on schools such as ours. Being a member of EAS has helped me to feel more comfortable and justified in doing so. An incident that illustrates the power that can come from simply communicating with others across the district took place this past spring.
>
> Since the passage of California's Proposition 227, parents who would like to have their children in a bilingual program are required to sign a waiver, which exempts the school from the requirement to teach their children in the English language exclusively. Due to the pressure to have students move more quickly into all-English instruction, the waiver-signing process at my site has become more hidden and difficult for parents. This year, waivers were available

at the night meeting of the council for parents of English language
learners and two daytime meetings. The fact that waivers would
be available to sign at the night meeting was not advertised, and
the daytime meetings were held in late spring, when most parents
have returned to work in the strawberry fields. In addition, when
parents went directly to the office to sign waivers, they were often
told (even by the principal) that the staff person trained in explaining
the waiver process was not available. One of the parents of a child
in my class—a parent who had spent nearly every day during the
winter months when she was not working in the strawberry fields
volunteering in my classroom—came to me with tears in her eyes,
as she was so frustrated at not being able to get to the school at
the designated hours. When I asked if she could come during her
lunch break, she told me that she only had a half-hour lunch and was
picking at a remote location where she was taken by bus.

My complaints to my school administration about this situation
were met with defensiveness, and no action was taken in response to
my concerns. Other bilingual teachers on staff, although concerned,
were not angry or motivated to complain, but saw this as just one
more nail in the coffin of our bilingual program, something they had
seen coming. It was at this point that I happened to tell this story at
an EAS meeting. Finally, there, I found the reaction that matched the
outrage I was feeling. EAS members were angry, incredulous, ready
to support me, and even ready to take action themselves. Most helpful
was a member from another early-exit program school who outlined
the way the waiver process is advertised and carried out at her site.
Armed with this information and support, I returned to my school the
next week, and requested another evening waiver meeting, which
was arranged. Better still, I've asked that our school investigate the
way waivers are made available at the other early-exit school where
my EAS colleague teaches.

Our network of support encompasses other groups who share our commitments. Because we are part of the Working Conditions Subcommittee of
our local union, we have been able to call upon the union for support. Our
initiatives have received union endorsement before going public, which has
expanded the scale and scope of our group's actions as well as adding to the
group's legitimacy. Of course, this is possible because in the last few years
our local union affiliate is committed to making sure that teachers have a
voice when it comes to developing and implementing educational policy. We
have also made similar connections with a community-based organization
comprised of teachers, parents, and other community members that was

also established in 2007. This group has focused on improving communication and action for parent and student advocacy.

In order to ensure that EAS is a safe space, we have tried to respect the wishes and voices of others. This is most evident in our efforts to honor group members' requests to maintain their anonymity. This desire has intensified in the current climate of budget shortfalls and teacher layoffs. We must be responsive to this concern if we are to continue functioning as a group. Thus far, we have been able to engage in public acts that contest institutional authority in anonymous ways without suffering consequences. This has included making sure that those teachers wishing to do so can endorse statements that appear in the newspaper without revealing their identity and using the union to disseminate and elicit support for our views and actions.

We have also faced challenges in our efforts to work as a group. Because we lead busy lives and have many responsibilities, making it hard to sustain our work as a group, attendance at our meetings is uneven. Former and current group members have also voiced concerns that the group doesn't do enough. We don't always pursue actions that we've discussed or recommended. We hope to address this concern by making sure that our meetings are facilitated in a way that ensures the involvement of all and includes time for identifying actions, setting priorities, assigning tasks to group members, and establishing deadlines.

EAS emerged as we came together to name, understand, and address a policy context that has prevented us from assuming our role as the professional stewards responsible for meeting the academic needs of our students. In mitigating the isolation and lack of autonomy we were experiencing at our school sites, we made sure that EAS was a safe space where each individual's voice and personal choices were respected. This has entailed creating an environment where new and veteran teachers can participate without having to reveal their identity. As we have worked together in this safe space, we have mobilized and benefited from the diverse set of experiences, professional knowledge, and contacts that each of us possesses. As a collective, we have also established connections with like-minded organizations in our region. Through our collective endeavors, EAS has become a network that continues to offer problem solving support for individuals as site- and district-based issues arise, both at meetings, and through the password-protected Web dialogue. This kind of network provides a supportive professional community that counters the isolation teachers are experiencing in the current policy context.

Note: Most names in this chapter are fictitious to protect anonymity.

References

Ackoff, L., & Greenberg, D. (2008). The objective of education is learning, not teaching. *Turning learning right side up: Putting education back on track.* Upper Saddle River, NJ: Pearson.

Akiba, M., & LeTendre, G. (2009). *Improving teacher quality.* New York: Teachers College Press.

Anyon, J. (2005). *Radical possibilities.* New York: Routledge.

Au, W. (2007). High-stakes testing and curricular control: A qualitative metasynthesis. *Educational Researcher, 36*(5), 258–267.

Berry, W. (1977). *The unsettling of America: Culture & agriculture.* New York: Avon.

Bigelow, B. (2009). Standards and tests attack multiculturalism. In W. Au (Ed.), *Rethinking multicultural education* (pp. 53–62). Milwaukee, WI: A Rethinking Schools Publication.

Bishop, R., & Berryman, M. (2006). *Culture speaks: Cultural relationships and classroom learning.* Wellington, Aotearoa, New Zealand: HUIA Publishers.

Bloom, H. S., Ham, S., Melton, L., & O'Brien, L. (2001). *Evaluating the accelerated schools approach: A look at early implementation and impacts on student achievement in eight elementary schools.* New York: Manpower Demonstration Research Corporation.

Cahnmann, M. S., & Remillard, J. T. (2002). What counts and how: Mathematics teaching in culturally, linguistically, and socioeconomically diverse urban settings. *Urban Review, 34*(3), 179–204.

Carter, C., & Osler, A. (2000). Human rights, identities and conflict management: A study of school culture as experienced through classroom relationships. *Cambridge Journal of Education, 30*, 335–356.

Caudet, F. (1987). *Antonio Machado para niños.* Madrid: Ediciones de la Torre, Colección Alba y mayo, Serie Poesía.

Christensen, L. (2009). *Teaching for joy and justice: Re-imagining the language arts classroom.* Milwaukee, WI: Rethinking Schools, Ltd.

Cisneros, S. (1991). *The house on Mango street.* New York: Vintage.

Cohen, E., & Lotan, R. (Eds.). (1997). *Working for equity in heterogeneous classrooms.* New York: Teachers College Press.

Comer, J. P. (1988). Educating poor minority children. *Scientific American, 259* (5), 42–48.

Cook-Saither, A. (2006). Sound, presence, and power: "Student voice" in educational research and reform. *Curriculum Inquiry, 36*(4), 359–390.

Cornbleth, C. (1995). Curriculum knowledge: Controlling the "great speckled bird." *Educational Review, 47*(2), 157–164.

Delpit, L. (1995). *Other people's children*. New York: Free Press.

Derman-Sparks, L., & the Anti-Bias Task Force. (1989). *Anti-bias curriculum: Tools for empowering young people*. Washington, DC: National Association for the Education of Young Children.

Dewey, J. (1944). *Democracy and education*. New York: Free Press.

Diamond, J. B., Randolph, A., & Spillane, J. P. (2004). Teachers' expectations and sense of responsibility for student learning: The importance of race, class, and organizational habitus. *Anthropology & Education Quarterly, 35*(1), 75–98.

Donnell, K. (2007). Getting to we: Developing transformative urban teaching practice. *Urban Education, 42*(3), 223–249.

Dudley-Marlin, C. (2005). Disrespecting teachers: Troubling developments in reading instruction. *English Education, 37*(4), 272–279.

Ehlert, L. (1989). *Eating the alphabet*. San Diego: Harcourt Brace.

Fine, M., Weis, L., & Powell, L. C. (1997). Communities of difference: A critical look at desegregated spaces created for and by youth. *Harvard Educational Review, 67*(2), 247–285.

Freire, P. (1998). *Pedagogy of freedom*. Lanham, MD: Rowman & Littlefield.

García, O., Kleifgen, J. A., & Falchi, L. (2008). *From English language learners to emergent bilinguals*. New York: The Campaign for the Educational Equity, Teachers College, Columbia University.

Gay, G. (2000). *Culturally responsive teaching: Theory, research, and practice*. New York: Teachers College Press.

Ginwright, S. A. (2010). *Black youth rising: Activism and racial healing in urban America*. New York: Teachers College Press.

González, N., Moll, L., & Amanti, C. (Eds.). (2005). *Funds of knowledge: Theorizing practices in households and classrooms*. Mahwah, NJ: Lawrence Erlbaum.

Gutstein, E., Lipman, P., Hernandez, P., & de los Reyes, R. (1997). Culturally relevant mathematics teaching in a Mexican American context. *Journal for Research in Mathematics Education, 28*(6), 709–737.

Hagiwara, S., & Wray, S. (2009). Transfer in reverse: Naïve assumptions of an urban educator. *Education and Urban Society, 42*(3), 338–363.

Hauser-Cram, P., Sirin, S. R., & Stipek, D. (2003). When teachers' and parents' values differ: Teachers' ratings of academic competence in children from low-income families. *Journal of Educational Psychology, 95*(4), 813–820.

Irvine, J. J. (2003). *Educating teachers for diversity: Seeing with a cultural eye*. New York: Teachers College Press.

Irvine, J. J., & Armento, B. J. (2001). *Culturally responsive teaching: Lesson planning for elementary and middle grades*. Boston: McGraw-Hill.

Jimenez, F. (2002). *Cajas de cartón*. New York: Houghton Mifflin Harcourt.

Johnson, E. (1881). *Legends, traditions and laws of the Iroquois or Six Nations and history of the Tuscarora Indians*. Lockport, NY: Union Printing and Publishing Co.

Joyce, B., & Showers, B. (2002). *Student achievement through staff development.* Alexandria, VA: ASCD.

Kesey, K. (1962). *One flew over the cuckoo's nest.* New York: New American Library.

Krull, K. (2003). *Harvesting hope: The story of Cesar Chavez.* San Diego: Harcourt.

Ladson-Billings, G. (1994). *The dreamkeepers: Successful teachers of African American children.* San Francisco: Jossey-Bass.

Ladson-Billings, G. (1995). Toward a theory of culturally relevant pedagogy. *American Educational Research Journal, 32*(3), 465–491.

Levin, H. M. (1988). *Accelerated schools for at-risk students.* New Brunswick, NJ: Center for Policy Research in Education.

Lieberman, A., & Pointer Mace, D. (2008). Teacher learning: The key to educational reform. *Journal of Teacher Education, 59*(3), 226–234.

Lynn, M. (2006). Education for the community: Exploring the culturally responsive practices of black male teachers. *Teachers College Record, 108*(12), 2497–2522.

Manthey, G. (2006, November 1). More than just the facts: The California Content Standards emphasize factual knowledge, but with a touch of adaptive expertise, educators can encourage creativity in all subject areas. *The Free Library.* Retrieved December 22, 2009, from http://www.thefreelibrary.com/More than just the facts: the California Content Standards emphasize...-a0155401207

Marri, A. (2005). Building a framework for classroom-based multicultural democratic education: Learning from three skilled teachers. *Teachers College Record, 107*(5), 1036–1059. Retrieved August 14, 2009, from http://www.tcrecord.org

McCombs, B. L. (2003). A framework for the redesign of K–12 education in the context of current educational reform. *Theory into Practice, 42*(2), 93–101.

McLaughlin, M. W., Irby, M. A., & Langman, J. (1994). *Urban sanctuaries: Neighborhood organizations in the lives and futures of inner-city youth.* San Francisco: Jossey-Bass.

Meier, D. (2002). *In schools we trust.* Boston: Beacon Press.

Meier, D. (2004). NCLB and democracy. In D. Meier & G. Wood (Eds.), *Many children left behind* (pp. 66–78). Boston: Beacon Press.

Michie, G. (1999). *Holler if you hear me.* New York: Teachers College Press.

Miser, A. B. (2006). Connecting to the community: Speaking the truth without hesitation. In J. Landsman & C. W. Lewis (Eds.), *White teachers/diverse classrooms, a guide to building inclusive schools, promoting high expectations, and eliminating racism* (pp. 185–202). Sterling, VA: Stylus.

Nastasi, B. K., & Clements, D. H. (1991). Research on cooperative learning: Implications for practice. *School Psychology Review, 20*(1), 110–131.

National Center for Fair and Open Testing. (2007, December 17). What's wrong with standardized tests? Retrieved September 23, 2009, from http://www.fairtest.org

Newmann, F. M. (1990). Qualities of thoughtful social studies classes: An empirical profile. *Journal of Curriculum Studies, 22*(3), 253–275.

Nieto, S. (2003). Challenging current notions of "high qualified teachers" through work in a teachers' inquiry group. *Journal of Teacher Education 54*(5), 386–398.

Ogawa, R. T., Sandholtz, J. H., Martinez-Flores, M., & Scribner, S. P. (2003). The substantive and symbolic consequences of a district's standards-based curriculum. *American Educational Research Journal, 40* (1), 147–176.

Olivos, E. M. (2006). *The power of parents: A critical perspective of bicultural parent involvement in public schools* (Vol. 290). New York: Peter Lang.

Orwell, G. (1984). *Nineteen eighty-four.* New York: Oxford University Press. (Originally published in London: Secker & Warburg, 1949)

Pang, V. O., & Sablan, V. A. (1998). Teacher efficacy. In M. E. Dilworth (Ed.), *Being responsive to cultural differences* (pp. 39–58). Washington, DC: Corwin.

Perry, T., Steele, C., & Hilliard, A., III. (2003). *Young, gifted and Black.* Boston: Beacon Press.

Reyes, P., Scribner, J. D., & Scribner, A. P. (Eds.) (1999). *Lessons from high-performing Hispanic schools.* New York: Teachers College Press.

Rivera, T. (1996). *. . . y no se lo tragó la tierra.* Houston, TX: Arte Publico Press.

Ryan, W. (1976). *Blaming the victim.* New York: Vintage Books.

Santamaria, L. J. (2009). Culturally responsive differentiated instruction: Narrowing gaps between best pedagogical practices benefitting all learners. *Teachers College Record, 111*(1), 214–247.

Schultz, B. D. (2008). *Spectacular things happen along the way.* New York: Teachers College Press.

Sleeter, C. E. (2005). *Un-standardizing curriculum: Multicultural teaching in the standards-based classroom.* New York: Teachers College Press.

Soto, G. (1990). *A fire in my hands: A book of poems.* New York: Scholastic.

Stanley, J. (1992*). Children of the Dust Bowl: The true story of the school at Weedpatch Camp.* New York: Crown.

Stevenson, R. B. (1990). Engagement and cognitive challenge in thoughtful social studies classes: A study of student perspectives. *Journal of Curriculum Studies, 22*(4), 329–341.

Valenzuela, A. (1999). *Subtractive schooling.* Albany: State University of New York Press.

Villegas, A. M., & Lucas, T. (2002). *Educating culturally responsive teachers.* Albany: State University of New York Press.

Walqui, A. (2006). Scaffolding instruction for English language learners: A conceptual framework. *The International Journal of Bilingual Education and Bilingualism, 9*(2), 152–180.

Ware, F. (2006). Warm demander pedagogy: Culturally responsive teaching that supports a culture of achievement for African American students. *Urban Education, 41*(4), 427–456.

Warren, S. R. (2002). Stories from the classroom: How expectations and efficacy of diverse teachers affect the academic performance of children in poor urban schools. *Educational Horizons, 80*(3), 109–116.

Weiner, L. (1999). *Urban teaching: The essentials.* New York: Teachers College Press.

Yeo, F. L. (1997). *Inner-city schools, multiculturalism, and teacher education.* New York: Garland.

Index

Pease-Alvarez, L., 142
Pedagogy
    culturally appropriate. *See* Culturally
        responsive teaching
    novice teachers and, 12
    perfecting and refreshing, 22–23
    socially aware, 7–8
    teacher- versus student-centered,
        57–58, 83
    working creatively with, 57–59
People, connecting with, 26, 33.
    See also Community
Perea, J., 9, 59
    career overview, 73
    experiences and reflections, 73–81
Perry, T., 6
Persistence, 20–21
Photography, in student research
        projects, 78
Plant biology, in thematic unit, 66–68
Playground activities, engaging students
        during, 54
Poetry, writing about, 44–45
Pointer Mace, D., 126
Political issues, in socially aware
        teaching, 8
Poster activities, 89
Powell, L. C., 7
Prejudice, experience of, 51–52
Primeros Pasos (First Steps), 130
Problem-solving, 75–76
Professional development/support,
        81, 125–27
    assessment-based approach and,
        1–2
    Educators Advocating for Students as
        venue for, 149–50
    international comparisons, 126
Program improvement (PI) schools,
        143
Programme for International Student
        Assessment (PISA), 126
Public good, education for, 7, 8
Public-speaking contest
    coaching students for, 27–30
    post-school accomplishments and,
        29, 31

Racism, classroom discussions
    example, 47–48
    listening to, 36
    teacher's role in, 48–50
Ramirez, R., 142
Randolph, A., 6
Rapport with students, advantages of,
        32
Recess, engaging students during, 54
Reciprocal teaching, 136
Reflection, importance of, 103
Reflective practice, 137–38
Relevance. *See* Culturally responsive
        teaching
Remillard, J. T., 4
Research
    on culturally responsive teaching, 4
    on intellectual engagement, 6
    student projects, 76–77
Responsibility
    instilling in students, 75–77
    of teacher as intellectual leader,
        117–18
Rethinking Schools publications,
        134, 141
Reyes, P., 6
Richman, K., 9, 59
    career overview, 61
    experiences and reflections, 61–72
Rickard, C., 107
Rickard, E., 107
Rickard-Weinholtz, J., 9, 98
    career overview, 101
    experiences and reflections,
        101–13
Rights of the Child, UN Convention
        on, 7
Ringler, S., 142
Rivera, T., 119
Roberts, M., 36
    career overview, 47
    experiences and reflections,
        47–56
Rodriguez, F., 142
Rote memorization, learner-centered
        teaching versus, 5–6, 80
Ryan, W., 49

Sablan, V. A., 6
Sandholtz, J. H., 57
"Sandwich method," of discipline, 95
Santamaria, L. J., 4
Schultz, B. D., 11–12
Science, in thematic unit, 66–67
Scribner, A. P., 6
Scribner, J. D., 6
Scribner, S. P., 57
Scripted curriculum
    academic achievement and, 80–81
    challenges, 73–81
    teacher-bashing and, 125
Self-identity, validation of, 20, 21
Self-selected learning experiences,
    76–77
Showers, B., 130, 137
Sirin, S. R., 6
Sleeter, C. E., 2, 4, 49
Social change, working toward,
    121–22
Social promotion, 26
Social studies, incorporating in
    thematic unit, 68–70
Socially aware teaching, 7–8
Soto, G., 44–45
Sovereignty, 109
Specially Designed Academic
    Instruction in English (SDAIE),
    135–36
Spillane, J. P., 6
Standards-based approaches, 1–2. See
    also Scripted curriculum
    Educators Advocating for Students'
        resistance to, 9, 127, 142–53
    impact, 125
    memorization versus intellectual
        engagement, paradox of, 5
    multiculturalism and, 7
    research on effects, 57–58
Stanley, J., 69
Steele, C., 6
Stevenson, R. B., 6
Stiller, S., 9, 59
    career overview, 82
    experiences and reflections, 82–96
Stipek, D., 6

Student voice
    classroom community and, 55
    opening up, 36
    validation, 20
Students
    abilities of, working with, 86
    in group work, regaining attention
        of, 92–93
    learning to learn from, 35–36
    as researchers and writers, 77–79
    teacher attitudes toward, 84–86
Student-teacher relationship, 36
Support, for teachers, 81, 125–27

Teacher expectations
    student accomplishment and, 6, 83
    student race and class background,
        links between, 6
Teacher networking, 126
Teacher-bashing, 125
Teachers, 132
    attitudes toward students, 84–86
    becoming, reasons for, 16, 25, 38
    culturally responsive,
        characteristics of, 4
    learning to learn from students,
        35–36
    novice, mentoring of, 11
    outstanding. See Visionary teaching/
        teachers
    professional support for, 81
    as professionals, 132
    racism and, classroom discussions on,
        47–56
    staying as, reasons for, 23, 46, 72
Teachers' beliefs
    about parental expectations, 6, 97
    confronting own, 12
Teaching force, international
    comparisons, 125–26
Teaching moments
    discriminatory behavior, 51–52
    student identity used as, 20
    unexpected, flexibility and, 22
Teaching strategies
    assessment-based, impact of, 1–2
    reciprocal, 136

About the Editors

Christine E. Sleeter, Ph.D., is professor emerita in the College of Professional Studies at California State University–Monterey Bay, where she was a founding faculty member, and she is a visiting professor at San Francisco State University. She was formerly a high school learning disabilities teacher in Seattle. She is president of the National Association for Multicultural Education, and was vice president of Division K of the American Educational Research Association. Her research focuses on anti-racist multicultural education and multicultural teacher education. Dr. Sleeter has published more than 100 articles in edited books and journals such as *Journal of Teacher Education* and *Curriculum Inquiry*. Her recent books include *Critical Multiculturalism: Theory and Praxis* (with Stephen May, 2010) and *Doing Multicultural Education for Achievement and Equity* (with Carl Grant, 2007). She was recently awarded the American Educational Research Association Social Justice in Education Award.

Catherine Cornbleth is professor in the Graduate School of Education, University at Buffalo, State University of New York (SUNY), where she teaches graduate courses in curriculum and critical interpretations of research. She continues to work with prospective and newer as well as experienced teachers. Her 1994 journal article "Teachers in Teacher Education" (*American Educational Research Journal*, with Jeanne Ellsworth) won the 1995 American Association of Colleges for Teacher Education (AACTE) Outstanding Writing Award. A graduate of the Chicago public schools, she taught high school social studies in Texas and Connecticut before returning to graduate school. She has authored or co-authored several books, including *Curriculum in Context* (1990), *The Great Speckled Bird: Multicultural Politics and Education Policymaking* (1995, with Dexter Waugh), and *Diversity and the New Teacher* (2008). Her scholarly articles have been published in journals such as *American Educational Research Journal*, *Journal of Curriculum Studies*, *Teachers College Record*, and *Anthropology and Education Quarterly*.